How to Stay Alive in the Woods

How to Stay Alive
in the Woods

BRADFORD ANGIER

originally published as
Living Off the Country

Illustrated by Vena Angier

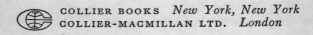

COLLIER BOOKS *New York, New York*
COLLIER-MACMILLAN LTD. *London*

First Collier Books Edition 1962

Seventeenth Printing 1973

How to Stay Alive in the Woods *originally appeared under the title* Living Off the Country: How to Stay Alive in the Woods

This Collier Books edition is published by arrangement with The Stackpole Company

The Macmillan Company
866 Third Avenue, New York, N.Y. 10022
Collier-Macmillan Canada Ltd., Toronto, Ontario

PRINTED IN THE UNITED STATES OF AMERICA

To my friend

COLONEL TOWNSEND WHELEN

who early began making marginal notes
on the book of nature, some of whose
most valuable chapters he is still writing.

Contents

Chapter

PART FOUR—SAFETY

PART ONE

SUSTENANCE

"A party living off the country must know how to get full value from everything available especially in the way of food."—*Royal Canadian Mounted Police*

Chapter 1

Every Necessity Is Free

ANYONE AT ANY TIME can suddenly find himself dependent on his own resources for survival. It costs very little time, money, and effort to be ready for such an emergency. If you are not ready, it may cost your life.

You may become lost or stranded in the woods. Thousands among North America's more than 30 million annually licensed fishermen and hunters do each year, many fatally. Yet almost invariably where such individuals suffer and all too often succumb so needlessly, wild food is free for the picking, meat for the taking, fire for the lighting, clothes for the making, and shelter for the satisfaction of building.

You may be in an automobile that is stalled by mishap or storm in an unsettled area, a not uncommon occurrence that frequently results in unnecessary hardship and tragedy. Perhaps you'll be a passenger in an aircraft that has to make a forced landing. Perhaps you'll be shipwrecked.

It may even happen that you and yours will be compelled to seek sanctuary in the wilderness because of those ever increasing threats to civilization itself—an atom bomb catastrophe or the even more terrible microscopic foes of germ warfare.

"Man's capacities have never been measured; nor are we to judge what we can do by any precedents, so little has been tried," pointed Thoreau. "What people say you can not do, you try and find you can."

No hard and fast rules can be laid down for survival anywhere, particularly in the farther places. Conditions vary. So do localities. Especially do individuals. Initiative on the other hand may be guided by a consideration of general principles such as those we can here absorb.

Many of the pitfalls, too, may be so recognized and evaded that otherwise might have to be learned by unnecessarily hard and often dangerous personal experience. It will be far more satisfactory to deal with natural difficulties by adaptation and avoidance than by attempting to overcome them by force.

Using the ways of living off the country discussed herein as a foundation for ingenuity and common sense, anybody who suddenly finds himself dependent upon his own resources will have a better chance both to keep living and to walk away from any hardships smiling.

The wilderness is too big to fight. Yet for those of us who'll take advantage of what it freely offers, nature will furnish every necessity. These necessaries are food, warmth, shelter, and clothing.

Chapter 2

Living Off The Country

ONE DAY YOU may be boating down the Peace River near the start of its more than 2000 mile journey, inland to Great Slave Lake and thence as the Mackenzie to the Arctic Ocean. Soon after the headwaters of this wilderness highway mingle in the Continental Trough, the river turns abruptly eastward to flow with surprising tranquility through the entire range of the Rocky Mountains. If you will watch the left shore after chuting through the minor turbulence known as Finlay Rapids, your eyes will likely as not catch the platinum gleam of Lost Cabin Creek.

Here it was at the turn of the century, during those apical days on the world's gold-fever chart, that four prospectors shared the cabin from which the stream has taken its name. Their grubstake dwindling, three watched with growing helplessness the first of their number die, by which time the survivors themselves had become so feeble that they lacked the vigor to open the frozen ground outside.

They buried their companion in the only spot they could find earth still loose enough to dig. A second prospector died and had also to be there interred. Before the fourth succumbed, he had by himself managed to scoop out enough of a grave so that a third emaciated body could join the others already beneath the cabin floor.

Yet as you will be able to testify from what you can see while boating past Lost Cabin Creek, and as I can substantiate from having camped there on several occasions, the vicinity abounds the year around with wild edibles.

Sustenance in the Silent Places

Starvation is not a great deal more pleasant than most of us would expect. The body becomes auto-cannibalistic after a few foodless hours. The carbohydrates in the system are devoured first. The fats follow.

This might not be too disagreeable, inasmuch as reducing diets seek to accomplish much the same result, but then proteins from muscles and tendons are consumed to maintain the dwindling strength their loss more gravely weakens.

No reasonable nourishment should therefore be scorned if one needs food. The Pilgrims derived considerable nutriment during their first desperate Massachusetts winter from groundnuts which are similar to small potatoes. Some northern explorers including Richardson, Franklin, and members of their parties lived for weeks and sometimes months almost entirely on the lichen known as rock tripe.

Wild turnips kept up John Colter's strength when the mountain man made his notable escape from the Indians. Beaver meat was a main item on the menu while Samuel Black explored the Finlay River. When regular rations on the Lewis and Clark expedition had to be reduced to one biscuit a day, it was the sweet yellow fruit of the papaw tree that kept the men going.

There is no need to explain why if any of us are ever stranded and hungry in the wilderness, we will want to start while our strentgh is near its maximum not to pass up any promising sources of sustenance.

Food Prejudices

Few will disagree, at least not when the moment of decision is at hand, that there is a point where luxuries as such become relatively unimportant.

One of the luxuries which we esteem most highly is the freedom to indulge our taste prejudices. These taste prejudices, a better understanding of which may one day prove beneficial, are commonly based on two factors.

First: there is a human tendency to look down upon certain foods as being beneath one's social station. Where grouse have been particularly thick in the Northeast, I've seen them scorned among backwoodsmen as a "poor man's dish." The same season in the Northwest where there happened to be a scarcity of grouse but numerous varying hares, the former were esteemed while I heard habitants apologizing for having rabbits in their pots. As it is everywhere in such matters, the lower the often self-designated station in life is, the more pronounced such evaluations become.

Second: it is natural to like the food to which we become accustomed. We in the United States and Canada have our wheat. The Mexican has his corn, the Oriental his rice. These grains we like also, but it would seem a hardship to have to eat them every day as we do wheat bread.

Our fastidiousness, too, is perhaps repelled by the idea of a Polynesian's eating raw fish, although at the moment we may be twirling a raw oyster in grated horseradish. The Eskimo enjoys fish mellowed by age. Many of us regard as choice some particularly moldy, odoriferous cheeses.

What About Frogs

Frog meat is one example of often disdained foodstuffs, so expensive in the sometimes more fashionable dining salons of the world, that nature furnishes free for the taking. The amphibians can be hooked with fishing tackle and small fly. They can be caught with string and bit of cloth, the former being given a quick tug when the latter is taken experimentally into the mouth.

Frogs can be secured with spears of various types. A sharpened stick will do. They can be so occupied at night by a light that you'll be able to net them and, even, occasionally to reach cautiously around and clamp a hand over one.

Most of the delicately flavored meat is on the hind legs

which can be cut off, skinned, and in the absence of cooking utensils extended over hot coals on a green stick for broiling. If rations were scant, you'd use the entire skinned frog after probably removing or at least emptying and cleaning the entrails, perhaps boiling the meat briefly with some wild greens.

Letting Predators Hunt For Us

If one of us is ever stranded and hungry, it may not be amiss to watch for owls, for spying one roosting in a quiet shadowy spot is not unusual, and it may be possible to steal close enough to knock it down. Although not as large and plump as would seem from outward appearances, an owl nevertheless is excellent eating.

What is more likely, however, is that we may scare an owl from a kill and thus secure ourselves a fresh supper. We may also have such good fortune, perhaps earlier in the day, with other predatory birds such as hawks and eagles. It is not uncommon to come upon one of these which has just captured a partridge. hare, or other prey that is proving awkward to lift from the ground, and by running to drive the hunter away with its talons empty.

Can Live Meat Be Overheated

Wolves, coyotes, and foxes may also be surprised at fresh kills that are still fit for human consumption. Such carnivora will seek new whereabouts at the sight or scent of an approaching human being.

One often hears it suggested that when any bird or animal has been unduly harassed before death, as may be considered to be the case if for example it has been relayed by wolves, its meat is not fit to eat. Such conclusions, however commendable their interpretation, arise usually from fashion more than from fact, although it is true that the appreciable amounts of lactic acid in such tissues do increase the rate of spoilage.

But it was because of this very characteristic, the fact that acids released by such stimuli as prolonged fatigue and fright make meat more tender, that not so long ago it was an unpleasant custom of the civilized world to make sure that animals killed for their meat died neither swiftly nor easily when either could be prevented.

How About Bears

Coming up to a bear's kill may be something else again. A wild bear probably won't dispute your presence. Then again it may, and although the chances are very much against this latter possibility, that is all the more reason not to take disproportionate risks.

If you are unarmed and really need the bear's meal, you will want to plan and execute your campaign with all reasonable caution. This will probably mean, first of all, spotting with the minutest detail preferably at least two paths of escape in case a fast exit should become advisable. This should not be too difficult where there are small trees to climb.

You'll then watch your opportunity and if for instance the kill is a still warm moose calf perhaps build a large fire beside it, discreetly gathering enough fuel to last for several hours; until morning if night be close at hand. You will take care in any event to be constantly alert until well away from the locality, realizing that bears, especially when they have gorged themselves, have a habit of dropping down near their food.

If you have a gun, you will be able to judge for yourself if the best procedure may not be to bag the bear itself. Fat for several reasons later discussed, becomes the most important single item in most survival diets, and the bear is particularly well fortified with this throughout most of the year. Except usually for a short period in the spring, bear flesh is therefore particularly nourishing.

Many, most of whom have never tasted bear meat nor smelled it cooking are prejudiced against the carnivore as a table delicacy for one reason or another. One excuse often heard concerns the animal's eating habits. Yet the most ravenous bear is a finicky diner when compared to such offerings as lobster and chicken.

It is only natural that preferences should vary, and if only for this reason it may be interesting to note:

(a) That many of our close acquaintances who live on wild meat much of the time relish plump bear more than any other North American game meat with the single exception of sheep,

(b) and that, furthermore, these individuals include a sizable number who after long professing an inability to stomach bear meat in any form found themselves coming back for thirds and even fourths of bear roast or bear stew under the impression that anything so savory must be, at the very least, choice beef.

Getting Birds Without Guns

Game birds such as ptarmigan and grouse promise feasts for anybody lost in the wilderness, especially as a few stones or sticks are often the only weapons needed. If one misses the first time, such fowl usually will afford a second and even a third try. When they do fly, they generally go only short distances and may be successfully followed, particularly if this is done casually and at such a tangent that it would seem that one were going to stroll on past.

Although it goes without saying that no sportsman will find any amusement in indiscriminate killing, it follows with equal reason that under survival conditions when wild meat may mean life itself such otherwise distasteful procedures will be justified by their success, even though regrets for their necessity may remain.

Any bird, as a matter of fact, will furnish good eating in an emergency. The only difference is that some are tenderer, plumper, and to different palates better flavored than others. Colonies afford particular opportunities, some of which are considered in Chapter 7. Even the riper eggs often obtainable should not be overlooked when one needs food.

Why Porcupines Are Given Reprieves

Porcupines, like thistles and nettles, are better eating than it might seem reasonable to expect. The slow moving, dull witted rodent is in human estimation often a nuisance, being so ravenous for salt that practically anything touched by human hands will whenever possible be investigated by sharp inquisitive teeth.

When shooting the rocky headwaters of the Southwest Miramichi River in New Brunswick, I've had to hunch out of my sleeping robe a half-dozen times a night to switch determined brown porkies away from my canvas canoe. Several years later. King Gething told me how when boating mail in the Canadian Rockies he'd solved with better success a similar problem. looping wires harmlessly around the yellowish necks of offending western hedgehogs and hitching them to poplars until he was ready to go the next morning.

The sluggish porcupine is the one animal that even the greenest tenderfoot. though weak with hunger, can kill with a weapon no more formidable than a stick. All one usually has to do thus to collect a meal is reach over the animal, which generally presents the raised quills of back and tail, and strike it on the head. Being so low in intelligence, the hedgehog requires a lot more killing than might be expected.

Porcupines can not, of course, shoot their quills, but any that are stuck in the flesh by contact should be pulled out immediately, for their barbed tips cause them to be gradually worked in out of sight. Dogs are common victims. I had a big Irish Wolfhound who became so infuriated at the genus that with no regard for himself, until later, he killed every porcupine he could find.

If you're alone in the bush with a dog in such a disagreeable predicament for all involved, you'll probably have to do as I did; lash the pet as motionless as possible against a tree, and use your weight for any necessary additional leverage. Pincers can be improvised by splitting a short branch, At any rate, each of the perhaps hundreds of quills has to come out, or death may be the least painful result.

This danger from quills is one reason why it is a poor practice to cook a porcupine by tossing it into a small fire. Very often all the quills are not burned off. Even if they are a considerable amount of fat will no doubt be consumed as well.

The best procedure is to skin out the porcupine, first turning it over so as to make the initial incision along the smooth underneath portion. Many who've dined on this meat consider the surprisingly large liver uncommonly toothsome.

The Most Widely Hunted Game Animal

In the spring particularly those years when rabbit cycles are near their zeniths, the young lie so fearlessly that a dog will step over one without scenting it, and all an individual has to do, if he wants, is to reach down and pick the youngster up.

Adult rabbits themselves depend so much on camouflage that at any time if you pretend not to see one and continue strolling as if going past, it is frequently possible to come close enough to do some immediately accurate throwing with a ready stone.

Tularemia is occasionally a threat in some localities and in one respect the disease is a little harder to avoid when not hunting with a firearm, for one precaution can be to shoot only rabbits that appear to be lively and in good health. The germs of rabbit fever are destroyed by heat, however, and another safeguard is to handle the animal with covered hands until the meat is thoroughly cooked.

Rabbits are unusually easy to clean. One method you may already use is commenced by pinching up enough of the loose back skin to slit by shoving a knife through. Insert your fingers and tear the fragile skin apart completely around the rabbit. Now peel back the lower half like a glove, disjointing the tail when you come to it and finally cutting off each hind foot. Do the same thing with the top section of skin, loosening it finally by severing the head and two forefeet. You can then, as you've very possibly found, pull the animal open just below the ribs and flip out the entrails, retrieving heart and liver. You may also want to cut out the small waxy gland between each front leg and body.

Starvation Next to Impossible

"It is next to impossible to starve in a wilderness," says George Leopard Herter, of Herter's, Inc., sporting goods manufacturer, importer, and exporter. "If no game, fish, mollusk, etc. are present, you are still in no danger.

"Insects are wonderful food, being mostly fat, and far more strengthening than either fish or meat. It does not take many insects to keep you fit. Do not be squeamish about eating insects, as it is entirely uncalled for. In parts of Mexico, the most nutritious flour is made from the eggs of small insects found in the marshes. In Japan, darning needles or dragon flies are a delicacy. They have a delicious delicate taste, so be sure to try them.

"Moths, mayflies, in fact about all the insects found in the woods, are very palatable. The only ones I ever found that I did not care for were ants. They contain formic acid and have a bitter taste. A small light at night will get you all the insects you need to keep you in good condition. If the weather is too cold for flying insects, kick open some rotten logs or look under stones and get some grubs. They keep bears fat and healthy and will do the same for you."

Odd Meals

Grasshoppers are edible when hard portions such as wings and legs have been removed. So are cicadas. Termites, locusts, and crickets are similarly eaten.

Both lizards and snakes are not only digestible but are often considered delicacies for which some willingly pay many times the amount they expend for a similar weight of prime beef. The only time snake meat may be poisonous is when it has suffered a venomous bite, perhaps from its own fangs. This also holds true with lizards, the only poisonous ones on this continent being the Southwest's Gila monster and Mexico's beaded lizard. To prepare the reptiles; decapitate, skin, remove the entrails, and cook like chicken to whose white meat the somewhat fibrous flesh is often compared.

Some aborigines have capitalized on the ants' acidity by mashing them in water sweetened with berries or sap to make a sort of lemonade. The eggs and the young of the ant are also eaten.

An ancient method for securing already cooked insects, reptiles, and small animals is to fire large tracts of grassland

and then to comb them for whatever may have been roasted by the conflagration.

A Rule for Survival

Although it is true that under ideal conditions the human body can sometimes fend off starvation for upwards of two months by living on its own tissues, it is equally certain that such auto-cannibalism is seldom necessary anywhere in the North American wilderness.

A good rule is not to pass up any reasonable food sources if we are ever in need. There are many dead men who, through ignorance or fastidiousness, did.

Chapter 3

Science Of Staying Alive

SOME NATIVES ROAST the bland young antlers of the deer family when these are in velvet. Others esteem the stomach contents of herbivorous mammals such as caribou, for such greens mixed as they are with digestive acids are not too unlike salad prepared with vinegar.

Some aborigines, as desirous of wasting nothing as those packers who can whole sardines, do not bother to open the smaller birds and animals they secure, but pound them to a pulp which is tossed in its entirety into the pot. Other peoples gather moose and rabbit excrement for thickening boiled dishes. Even such an unlikely ingredient as gall has, among other uses, utility as a seasoning.

Nearly every part of North American animals is edible. An occasional exception is polar bear and ringed and bearded seal liver which become so excessively rich in Vitamin A that they are poisonous to some degree at certain times and are usually as well avoided. All freshwater fish are likewise good to eat.

When natives refuse to partake of any or all of such fauna, the reason is often involved with tribal superstitions rather than edibility. Across the Peace River from our home site, to give an example, Dokie was returning to Moberly Lake with Harry Garbitt. The weather-rusted fare of the onetime chief corrugated with increasing dismay, as he watched the sourdough trader begin to cook the evening meal.

"No eatum whitefish," protested Dokie, and in the next breath, he explained why. "Whitefish me!"

"Okay," the philosophical Scotsman agreed. "Supper's over."

Why Blood Should Be Saved

Animals should not be bled any more than can be helped if food is scarce. Whether they should be so handled at other times is a matter largely of circumstances and of personal opinion.

Blood, which is not far removed from milk, is unusually rich in easily absorbed minerals and vitamins. Our bodies, for illustration, need iron. It would require the assimilation of ten ordinary eggs, we are told, to supply one man's normal daily requirements. Four tablespoons of blood are capable of doing the same job.

Fresh blood can be secured and carried, in the absence of handier means, in a bag improvised from one or another parts of the entrails. One way to use it is in broths and soups, enlivened perhaps by a wild vegetable or two.

Leather and Rawhide both Edible

The skin of the animal is as nourishing as a similar quantity of lean meat. Baking a catch in its hide, although ordinarily both a handy and tasty method of occasionally preparing camp meat, is therefore a practice we should not indulge in when rations are scarce.

Rawhide is also high in protein. Boiled, it has even less flavor than roasted antlers, and the not overly appealing and yet scarcely unpleasant look and feel of the boiled skin of a large fish. When it is raw, a usual procedure naturally enough adopted in emergencies is to chew on a small bit until mastication becomes tiresome and then to swallow the slippery shred.

Explorers speak of variances of opinion among individual members of groups as to whether or not leather, generally footwear or other body covering, should be eaten. When we are so situated that to reach safety we will probably have to walk, foot protection should of course come first. If we are cold as well as hungry, we will stay warmer by wearing the rawhide than we could by sacrificing it to obtain momentarily a little additional heat via the digestive system. If the article in question is made of commercially tanned leather, the answer will be simpler indeed, for such leather generally has scant if any food value.

Bones May Mean Salvation

A lot of us, when we have the time, capitalize in two different ways on the food value inherent in bones. Small bones go into the pot to thicken stews and soups, and we may also like to chew on the softer of these, particularly if we are lounging around a campfire. Larger marrow bones are opened so that their soft vascular tissue can be extracted.

The mineral-rich marrow found in the bones of animals that were in good physical condition at demise is not surpassed by any other natural food in caloric strength. What is, at the same time, the most delectable of tidbits is wasted by the common outdoor practice of roasting such bones until they are on the point of crumbling. A more conservative procedure is to crack them at the onset, with two stones if nothing handier is available. The less the marrow is then cooked, the better it will remain as far as nutrition is concerned.

All this is something to consider, assuredly, if any of us when desperate for food happens upon perhaps temporary salvation in the form of the skeleton of a large animal.

Rare or Well Done

When food supplies are limited, nothing should be cooked longer than is considered necessary for palatableness. The only exception is when there may be germs or parasites to be destroyed.

The more food is subjected to heat, the greater are the losses of nutritive values. Even the practice of making toast diminishes both bread's proteins and digestibility. The greatest single universal error made in preparing venison and similar game meat for the table is overcooking which, in addition to drying it out, tends to make it tough and stringy. What this practice does to the flavor is a matter of opinion.

Scurvy Easily Prevented and Cured

A very definite danger risked when fresh food is habitually overcooked, especially under survival conditions, arises from the fact that oxidation destroys the inherent Vitamin C, lack of which in the diet causes scurvy.

Scurvy has gathered more explorers, pioneers, trappers, and prospectors to their fathers than can ever be reckoned, for it is a debilitating killer whose lethal subtleties through the centuries have too often been misinterpreted and misunderstood.

Scurvy, it is known now, is a deficiency disease. If you have it, taking Vitamin C into your system will cure you. Eating a little Vitamin C regularly will, indeed, keep you from having scurvy in the first place.

Free Vitamins

Spruce tea can be made, by steeping fresh evergreen needles in water, that will be as potent with the both preventative and curative ascorbic acid as the ordinary orange juice. This vitamin you can get even more directly by chewing the tender new needles, whose starchy green tips are particularly pleasant to eat in the spring.

Fresh meat will both prevent and cure scurvy. So will fresh fish. So will fresh fruits and vegetables, wild or otherwise. So will lime juice and lemon juice but, no matter how sour, only if they too are sufficiently new. The Vitamin C in all these is lessened and eventually destroyed by oxidation, by age, and incidently by salt.

How Rabbit Starvation Really Happens

A man can have all the rabbit meat he wants to eat and still perish. So-called rabbit starvation, as a matter of fact, is particularly well known in the Far North.

An exclusive diet of any lean meat, of which rabbit is a practical example, will cause digestive upset and diarrhea. Eating more and more rabbit, as one is impelled to do because of the increasing uneasiness of hunger, will only worsen the condition.

The diarrhea and the general discomfort will not be relieved unless fat is added to the diet. Death will follow, otherwise, within a few days. One would probably be better off on just water than on rabbit and water.

The Tremendous Importance of Fat

Why is fat so important an item in a survival diet? Part of the answer, as we have seen, lies in the fact that eating lean flesh without a sufficient amount of fat will kill us, an actuality that may seem astonishing, for in civilization we obtain numerous fats from a very great number of often unrecognized sources. These include butter, oleomargarine, lard, milk, cheese, bacon, salad oil, mayonnaise, various sauces, candy, nuts, ice cream, and the fatty contents of such staples as bread.

If in an emergency we have to subsist entirely on meat, the fat of course will have to come from the meat itself. The initial consideration in a meat diet, therefore, is fat. We're going to get enough relatively of the lean. Our best day by day guide as to proportions will be our own individual appetites, for after we have in the course of not too hurried meals eaten sufficient fat, no more will taste good.

Yet history tells of supposedly experienced men who, although starving, have burned vital fat to give nutritively inferior lean meat what seemed to them a more appetizing flavor—a suicidal error of which we, having learned better in an easier way, need never be guilty.

Cannibalism

It has always been, among all social levels of all peoples, that famishing human beings left to their own resources will devour everything even suspected of having food value and eventually will resort to cannibalism.

"It is rare, except in fiction, that men are killed to be eaten.

There are cases where a member of a party becomes so unsocial in his conduct towards the rest that by agreement he is killed; but if his body then is eaten it is not logically correct to say that he was killed for food," Vilhjalmur Stefansson says. "What does happen constantly is that those who have died of hunger, or of another cause, will be eaten. But long before cannibalism develops the party has eaten whatever is edible."

Some scientists, who point out that objections are psychological and sociological, declare abstractly that animal proteins are desirable in direct ratio with their chemical similarity to the eating organism, and that therefore for the fullest and easiest assimilation of flesh materials, human meat can hardly be equaled.

What to Kill for Food

Some member of the deer family is what anyone really bogged down in the North American wilderness is most apt to turn to for sustenance. The adult males, as any sportsman knows, are fattest just before the mating season which, varying according to species and climate, commences roughly in early autumn. The male then becomes progressively poorer. At the end of the rut, the prime male is practically without fat even in the normally rich marrows.

The mature female is the choice of the meat hunter once the rutting season is well under way. She remains the preference until approximately early spring. Then the male once more comes to the fore. Generally speaking, the older animals have more fat than the younger.

Tidbit of Old-Time Trappers

Beaver was something I had very much wanted to eat ever since reading when a boy Horace Kephart's regretful observation: "This tidbit of old-time trappers will be tasted by few of our generation, more's the pity." It was a lean black-haired trapper, Dan Macdonald, who gave me the opportunity some years later, and as beaver are one of the principal fur animals

along the upper Peace River I've been fortunate enou
able to enjoy *amisk* many times since.

The meat is so sustaining that anyone lost and hungry is
markedly fortunate to secure it. Beaver cuttings, indicating
presence of the amphibian, are easily recognized by the marks
of large sharp teeth that have kept on gnawing around and
around, biting continually deeper until the wood was severed.
Because beaver don't know how trees will fall, the animal is
occasionally found trapped beneath trunk and branches.

If you have a gun and enough time at your disposal to wait
for a sure shot, an often productive campaign is to steal to a
concealed vantage on the downward side of a beaver pond.
The furry animals may then be seen swimming perhaps and
shot in the head. If you have a choice and not much ammunition, wait to bag the biggest one you can. Beaver, the largest
rodents on this continent, weigh up to fifty pounds and more.

Beaver quarters seem almost incommensurably delicious
when you're hungry from outdoor exertion, although with the
larger adults the meat does, even though you may be reluctant
to heed it, have a tendency to become somewhat fibrous and
stringy when cooked. The meat has a distinctive taste and
odor somewhat resembling that of plump turkey. A sound idea
in an emergency is to supplement it with lean flesh such as
rabbit, so as to take the fullest possible advantage of the fat.

A beaver tail, as anyone will be able to testify upon seeing
one, looks surprisingly like a scaly black fish whose head has
been removed. Tails may be propped or hung near a cooking
fire whose heat will cause the rough black hide to puff and to
separate from the flesh, whereupon it can be peeled off in
large flakes.

The beaver tail is so full of nourishing oil, incidentally, that
if set too close to a blaze it will burn like a torch. The meat is
white and gelatinous, and rich enough that one finds himself
not wanting too much of it at a time.

What Parts of Meat to Eat

We will probably want to eat most of any animals we can
secure if short of food. This in a way may be a boon if only

because it will place some of us, perhaps for the first time, in a position to determine personally if among the parts ordinarily discarded are not, as many claim, the most delicious portions.

Some segments, as for example the liver whose abundance of Vitamin A has caused it to be recognized even among some primitive tribes as a specific cure for night blindness, contain in more concentrated form certain of the necessary food elements.

But any section of plump fresh meat is a complete diet in itself, affording all the necessary food ingredients even if we dine on nothing but fat rare steaks for week after month after year.

Chapter 4

Food In The Farther Places

ACTUAL HUNDREDS of wild foods enhance as might be expected the fields and woodlands, mountains and canyons, the deserts, shores, and certainly the swamplands.

Adding from season to season the recognition of a few more can be, as you've perhaps already discovered, an engrossing and practical hobby, as well as a way both thrifty and healthful of pleasantly introducing new delicacies to the table. Such acquired knowledge can even mean, in some unforeseen emergency, the difference between eating bountifully and starving.

How to Obtain Birch Syrup

"Heavenly concoction," Dudley Shaw promised one spring day up on the Peace River. "I'll stow a gimlet in my pack when I prowl up the first of the week to retrieve a couple of traps that got frozen in. Noble lap, birch syrup is. Glorious on flippers."

The old trapper, who as mentioned in *At Home in the Woods* is the happiest man Vena and I have ever known, left instructions about preparing some containers. These could have been improvised from birchbark itself, but tomato cans to which we attached wire bails worked out handily enough. Hung on nails driven above each tiny hole Dudley made with his gimlet, the bright buckets echoed with the dripping flow of watery sap. Wooden pegs could have secured the containers below ax gashes or holes bored with a knife.

"You'd better amble out this way regularly to see that these don't overflow," Dudley Shaw cautioned, eyes blinking good humoredly behind thick spectacles. "Keep the sap simmering cheerfully on back of the stove. Tons of steam have to come off."

Would the procedure hurt the trees?

"No, no." Our nearest neighbor shook his head. "The plunder will begin to bog down when the day cools, anyway. Then we'll whittle out pegs and drive them in to close the blinking holes. Everything will be noble."

Everything was, particularly the birch syrup. It wasn't as thick as it might have been, not even after a great deal of cooking. There also seemed to be an unfortunately small amount. Yet what remained was sweet, delicately spicy, and more than ordinarily delicious. If one is ever seeking emergency sustenance in the spring, birch syrup may be well worth the time and effort if only for its psychological lift.

A Spaghetti That Grows on Trees

The widely distributed birches have other culinary uses. The inner bark is especially sweet and sustaining, being credited with saving actual hundreds of lives under emergency conditions on this continent alone. This cambium is enjoyable raw. It is also bland enough either to chop into bits or to cut into spaghetti-like lengths for adding to soups and stews. It retains its aromatic spiciness even when dried for storing or carrying.

Young leaves and twigs, the soft formative tissue between wood and bark, and the thin bark covering the roots are all steeped in hot water to make a favorite backwoods tea. When we sip this beverage, which has the perfume and flavor of wintergreen, and are perhaps thus stimulated to recall the other virtues of the birch, it is difficult not to agree that particularly where civilization is near it is unfortunate whenever this harmonious tree is unnecessarily disfigured.

Its bark, enough of which can be pulled harmlessly off in small dry wisps by the fingers alone, is unexcelled for starting campfires under every sort of adverse condition. Great sections of the bark are valuable in the farther places as a flexible emergency waterproofing material. It will and does serve for utensils, shelters, that most graceful of watercraft, and even for clothing.

Forests of Food

The lodgepole pine, together with other pines, has an eatable inner bark that is preferred fresh by some and sun-dried by others. There are even those among us who claim it is at its best only when scraped from the south side of a young tree while the spring sap is rising.

The poplar's sweetish sap layer is also eaten both raw and cooked. This, too, lies between the wood and the outside bark, the latter being intensely bitter with salicin which for some reason is relished by beaver and moose and which is an ingredient in some tonics concocted for the benefit of mankind.

Piñon

Ever since we got the habit while living in New Mexico of improving crisp fall afternoons by gathering pine nuts in the bright Sangre de Cristo Mountains, piñons have been a favorite of ours. These soft delicate nuts, which resemble peanuts in appearance but which in comparison seem little heavier than solidified fluff, form in the cones of the short gnarled pines of the arid southwestern highlands. They are flavorful raw, even more delicious roasted, and have a delicately nutty sweetness when pounded into flour and baked.

Why You May Choose to Avoid Mushrooms

One concrete fact, especially when combined with several other actualities, seems enough to warrant the conclusion that one should avoid whenever possible turning to mushrooms for emergency food. Mushrooms have very little general food value. If you are not already an expert, the incurred risks will be far out of proportion to the possible gain.

No single practical test is recognized, unfortunately, by which all poisonous mushrooms can be detected. It is untrue that if silver boiled with mushrooms does not turn black, the fungi are necessarily edible. It is a false presumption that when the skin can be peeled from the cap, the specie is proved wholesome. It is not true that pink gills are evidence that the mushroom is good. It is incorrect that if salt rubbed on some part of the mushroom causes a color change, the fungus must be suitable for the table.

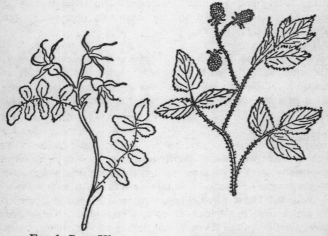

FIG. 1. Rose Hips.   FIG. 2. Raspberries.

Another dangerous fallacy, particularly under the stress of a fight for survival, is the apparently reasonable but nevertheless wholly false presumption that any mushroom gathered by animals and birds is suitable for human consumption. Among the mushrooms ordinarily harvested and dried by squirrels are some of the amanita group for which no antidote has been discovered.

So many myths are circulated, often by those who in their own neighborhoods successfully gather one or two types of edible mushrooms year after year, that it can not be here repeated too strenuously: no single test short of eating can distinguish between a poisonous and a safe mushroom.

As for puffballs, although it is correct that puffballs which are white throughout are edible when fresh, it is also true that some lethal mushrooms when young look like puffballs.

Mushrooms contain several different poisons. One small poisonous mushroom in an overflowing packsack of edible fungi can be enough to cause practically certain death, symptoms taking so long to become evident that once they are recognized, even the most immediate and complete hospital attention is often powerless. In the case of the Deadly Amanita, the individual may not realize anything is at all amiss until he is doubled up with cramps and vomiting, perhaps fifteen hours after eating the fatal toadstool.

Rose Hips

You probably can't think back to a time when you did not recognize the thorny vines and bushes of the wild rose, particularly when the frail flowers were achieving their sweetest fragrance. Can you remember when you weren't aware that from these blossoms develops a reddish orange, berrylike fruit that clings for months? Perhaps you can even recall when you first remarked how their delicate taste is reminiscent of domestic apples, another member of the rose family.

Rose hips can be a particularly valuable part of a wilderness diet because of their abundant Vitamin C which both averts and remedies scurvy. A lot of us get the habit, whenever hungry in the bush, of picking a few and nibbling the skin and flesh from around the seed-filled center.

Roses by Several Other Names

Other members of the rose family familiar by sight although not necessarily by name to almost everyone include blackberries, raspberries, salmonberries, dewberries, cloudberries, and thimbleberries. Even botanists sometimes have trouble in differentiating among the closely related species. All are composed of clusters of juicy little fruits, drawn together like a cap over a central head at the end of a stem. Each individual drupelet contains its own tiny seed. Ripened colors vary from salmons and reds through blacks. There is also considerable range in taste.

Animals particularly relish the leaves, stems, and stalks of certain species despite their barbs. In fact, a good place in many areas to look for deer during the opening hours of the season is in a raspberry patch, and just the other day we had a favorite thicket prematurely pruned when I thoughtlessly picketed our horses where they could nip at the bushes.

Anyone who'll take the trouble to peel and taste some of the young shoots will discover why, for they are a palatable emergency food in themselves. Young leaves, tossed into boiling water and set away from the fire to steep, make an agreeable frontier tea.

Peculiarities of the High-Bush Cranberry

This roundish red berry, like some of the more expensive hors d'oeuvres, usually requires a cultivated taste. You pop one of the bright little ovals into your mouth and bite down on it experimentally. The odd sourness perhaps constrains you

FIG. 3. High-bush Cranberries.

to spit it out. The flavor which remains, however, is provocative. You try again and, let us hope, again.

Then, as likely as not, you find yourself looking forward to the unusual tartness of the fruit. You are apt to come to appreciate it particularly when thirsty, for the juice from a mouthful of high-bush cranberries quenches dryness like no other wild berry I know. The usual procedure, as a matter of fact, is to burst the berry in the mouth and swallow the juice, thereafter expelling skin and flattish seeds.

At least a few high-bush cranberries remain on the bushes the year around, puckering as they dehydrate with age. Once one recognizes the shrub, its nearness is easy to detect by reason of its peculiar sweetish-sour odor. On sub-zero days, the berries melt against the tongue like sherbet. They also make a popular backwoods jelly that has none of the bitterness of the familiar vine cranberry.

One Drawback of Familiar Vine Cranberry

The firm red cranberry, which grows on thin vines which creep over innumerable acres of marsh and moist woodland,

FIG. 4. Saskatoon or Serviceberry.

is a familiar sight on fruit counters particularly around the Thanksgiving and Christmas holidays. The cranberry's only drawback as an emergency food is its unpalatable bitterness.

Stewed with an added sweet such as the blueberries that are often growing nearby, the cranberry's rightfully deserved popularity is more easy to recognize.

Frontiersmen still gather the wild fruit by the bushels, many whittling flat-bottom scoops with series of long V-shaped teeth so as to strip the vines more easily. It then becomes a pleasant evening occupation to help empty pails onto a stretched, slanted blanket. Leaves, stems, and other debris are thus caught and are later shaken away, while the ripe cranberries roll and bound into ready containers for later use in a variety of dishes ranging from pies to bannock.

Blueberries Thicken Soups

There are more than a score of different species of blueberries, also known in some localities as whortleberries and as huckleberries, some crowding tall bushes while others fill tiny shrubs only three or four inches from the ground.

Blueberries are historically one of the most valuable foods of Indians who have long eaten them as is, dried, with meat, as a thickening for soups, and in numerous other ways. Bushmen pick them by the bushel, often with the same sort of toothed scoop used for cranberries.

Other Wild Fruits

Other wild fruits are so obviously numerous that it is impractical to do more than mention a few. All of us might well make it our business to learn what edibles abound in our favorite woodlands and, if possible, in any wilderness area where we may one day travel.

The numerous gooseberries and currants are widely popular. Indians utilized dried currants extensively to flavor pemmican, which is essentially equal parts by weight of dried meat and rendered fat. The serviceberry is another fruit that was included in pemmican.

The younger one is, the more irresistible the various wild cherries seem to be, especially when raw. Adults come to prefer gathering the more astringent of these green for jelly making and ripe for boiling with an added sweet for table syrup.

Many of us have savored wild grapes and wild plums.

FIG. 5. Elderberries.

Elderberries are well known. The dry, bland, reddish bearberry is edible although practically tasteless. So are the equally innocuous berries of the kinnikinic whose leaves have been so often used instead of or to supplement dwindling tobacco supplies, that many other substitutes, such as the inner bark of the flowering dogwood, are also called kinnikinic.

The first wild berry I remember gathering was the dryish fruit of the little wintergreen which I used to find growing beneath pine trees in New Hampshire, where they were so scarce that I soon learned the evergreen leaves of this tiny plant have a similar flavor.

How to Test for Edibility

Innumerable edible wild fruits, barks, roots, seeds, flowers, pods, saps, gums, herbs, nuts, leaves, greens, and tubers are both nourishing and satisfying. The need for extreme discretion unless one is sure of what he is eating can not be overemphasized, however, as we all realize.

FIG. 6. Bearberry.

The possible gain in an absolute emergency might be important enough, in ratio to risk, that we would be justified in trying a very small sample of a strange plant, then if all went well a slightly larger sample, and so on. This process should be stretched over as long a period as reasonable, certainly no less than twenty-four hours, because of the slowness in which some poisons act.

During that time we'd be watching with as much detachment as we could muster for any ill effects. If everything seemed all right, we would then be justified if the emergency continued to consider the plant edible in at least small quantities.

Chapter 5

Yours For The Eating

"I LEARNED THAT a man may use as simple a diet as the animals, and yet retain health and strength. I have made a satisfactory dinner off a dish of purslane which I gathered and boiled," Henry Thoreau noted. "Yet men have come to such a pass that they frequently starve, not from want of necessaries but for want of luxuries."

The salad plants and potherbs growing wild on this continent, among which the trailing purslane with its yellow flowers is often regarded less highly than others, are so abundant that when one stays hungry for very long in the silent spaces it is not always with good reason.

No Charge for This Coffee

Very often in the spring, especially when this season follows a winter passed in the sub-zero tightness of some northern wilderness, we awake with the hankering to eat something new and green.

On many such days, in broadly separated parts of the continent, we've left at dawn with little aim except to find as many wild green vegetables as we could and perhaps to savor, at least until the sun rose higher, the good humor of Thoreau's contention: "Some would find fault with the morning red, if they got up early enough." Upon our return, there would likely as not be at least a few dandelions in my pack.

Almost all of us know this member of the chicory family, if only because of its persistency in dotting lawns with hollow-stemmed yellow flowers. The entire young plant is relished both raw in salads and, especially when older, after it had been boiled just long enough to become tender. The clean bitter tang is to many stimulating. Those who do not care for it can throw away the first water and finish the boiling in fresh fluid.

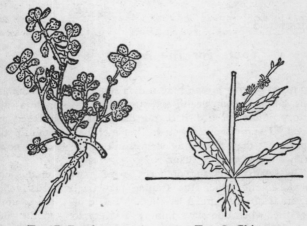

FIG. 7. Purslane.   FIG. 8. Chicory.

You may also care to gather a pan of roots, dry them, roast them in the oven, and finally grind the shriveled results. It is a universally used coffee stretcher and coffee substitute. Even more widely known in this respect are the similarly processed roots of the closely related chicory. Especially when young this is often mistaken for dandelion, as there is then little difference between the two except that chicory instead of being stemless has a stalk. Chicory later has a large, usually blue flower.

Pigweed By Several Other Names

Just as the succulent dark meat of the muskrat is sometimes better preferred when served as swamp rabbit, so is pigweed more attractive to many when called wild spinach or lamb's quarter. Its mild flavor and widespread prolificness make it one of the more important wild greens. The stem is covered with longish pale green leaves with irregular edges, whose shape has gained the wild vegetable the additional cognomen of goosefoot. The small green flowers appear in long thick clusters that turn later to tiny dark seeds.

Stalk, leaves, flowers, and grains are all nourishing both raw and cooked. Even when a small vegetable garden is in full production near our wilderness home, we often pass it to gather instead young pigweed growing nearby. For ourselves,

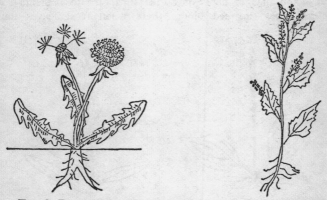

FIG. 9. Dandelion.   FIG. 10. Pigweed or Lamb's Quarter.

we know of no domestic green that equals it in taste, and although this is admittedly a matter of personal preference, it is interesting, to us at least, that many of our backwoods neighbors have similar opinions.

The seeds, like those of the green amaranth which is also called pigweed, go well to relieve whatever monotony there may be in bannock and other breadstuffs, lending them a caraway-seed effect. They can also be dried and ground for use as meal.

Plantain Is Good to Eat

An almost universally distributed weed that you no doubt know but perhaps never have considered as a food is plantain. This is the short stemless plant with broad green leaves rising, directly from the root, about a straight central spike. This projection blossoms with minute greenish flowers that later turn to seeds. The leaves of the herb cook up into greens.

Tea Is Also Free

Fireweed is another herb difficult to mistake, especially when the single multileaved stalks brighten with purplish flowers. Thousands of acres of burnt lands turn to magenta so thickly does fireweed bloom there when frost leaves the

FIG. 11. Plantain.   FIG. 12. Fireweed.

ground. The young stems when they first appear are tender enough to cook like asparagus. More mature stalks are peeled and their sweetish interiors eaten raw. The young leaves make passable greens.

Dried, fireweed leaves like those of plantain and many other eatables find their way into lone boiling kettles from which, after they have been infused, are poured beverages which their imbibers drink as tea.

All These and Nettles, Too

Nettles, possibly because they are such unlikely candidates for culinary endeavors, have become my favorite wild green vegetable. The nettle is another tall green herb hard to mistake, particularly as many who do not already recognize its food potentialities are all too well aware of the stinging hairs that ordinarily make this additional tea substitute something to be avoided.

Because of the nettles' irritating proclivities, the hands should be protected when nettles are gathered, preferably when they first appear in the spring. Leather gloves and a knife make the task easy. You can get along all right, too, by using two sticks as tongs.

It would be reasonable to expect that nettles would require lengthy cooking. As a matter of fact, you only have to drop the young shoots into a container of boiling water that may

FIG. 13. Nettle.   FIG. 14. Mustard.

be then set away from the heat. As soon as the dark emerald greens have cooled enough to be eaten, they may be forked out and served.

Table Mustard for the Making

Mustard, which thrives wild throughout most of the world, is familiar because of its brilliant yellow flowers that become almost solid masses along many fields and hillsides during spring and summer, and which in California I've seen equaling telephone poles in height.

Mustard is best as a green when it first appears. The young stalks from which leaves grow directly are not hard to recog-

FIG. 15. Clover.   FIG. 16. Miner's Lettuce.

nize, particularly as older mustard in bloom is often growing in the same patch. These slightly peppery leaves are enjoyed raw. So are the young yellow flowers. The entire plant goes well when cooked.

Table mustard can be made from the seeds by grinding them between two stones and adding enough water to make a paste. Commercially prepared condiments often contain such additional ingredients as flour, vinegar, salt, various spices, and occasionally horse-radish. The seeds are also used primitively for mixing with various meals and flours for flavoring.

Clover But Not Buttercups

Probably everyone has at some time sucked honey from the white, yellow, or reddish flowers of the clover. The sweetish roots are also appreciated, sometimes after first being smoked over a fire.

But just because a flowering plant may be familiar and to all external appearances not obnoxious, it does not necessarily follow that it is edible. A number of the equally familiar and apparently equally innocent buttercups are poisonous.

Miner's Lettuce

This salad plant, whose crisp leaves and stems may also be boiled as greens, is notably easy to distinguish. Anyone who does not know it already only has to look for a small green plant with flower stems growing from a short mass of leaves at ground level. The clinching feature is that partway up each

FIG. 17. Fertile Horsetail.   FIG. 18. Infertile Horsetail.

stem a pair of leaves grow together so as to form a sort of cup through whose middle the stalk continues.

The plant got its name because of a deserved popularity during gold rush days in California, when it was one of the fresh vegetables eaten to cure and to avert scurvy. We've enjoyed it here in the spring, gathering it in damp locations beneath the coastal pines.

Horsetail for Eating and Cleaning

Another virtually foolproof wild food, being especially easy to identify, is the horsetail. You've probably noticed this small green plant that flourishes in cool abundance about brooks, along shaded corduroyed toteroads, and in other damp locations; giving often the impression of a miniature evergreen forest and, again, of groves of whimsically dwarfed bamboos, for it exists in two different forms.

The infertile horsetail consists of a single stem, which resembles the trunk of a tiny pine tree all the more because of the green shoots that branch out from it in series of levels. The fertile horsetail thrusts up in one straight stem which ascends in joints which a lot of us have found ourselves pulling apart, junction by junction.

The fertile horsetail is also known as the scouring rush because the gritty surfaces of the older plants make them excellent articles to grab by the handful for use as scouring pads.

The outer tissue can be removed from the young shoots of the horsetail and the blandly sweet interiors eaten raw.

Cacti Furnish Food and Drink

The fruits and the fleshly sections of North American cacti are edible raw, boiled, roasted, stewed, and even fried. It is only important, as quickly becomes self-evident, that every caution be exerted in first removing the bristles and spikes, usually by heat or by cutting off the outer tissue.

A few of the larger and thicker plants are filled with enough watery sweetish juice to be vital under survival conditions for quenching thirst. If only because of this characteristic, tempered perhaps by the consideration that in rocky and sandy habitats a cactus takes so long to grow, it can be appreciated that the prickly plant should not ordinarily be damaged in arid country except in an emergency.

FIG. 19. Rock Tripe.

Nearly All Arctic Vegetation Eatable

All arctic vegetation is edible except for some mushrooms. This lethal species, which has white gills and a bulbous base, has a smooth top usually some three or four inches across when mature, and ranges in color from white and greenish white through greyish brown. To avoid poisonous mushrooms in the Arctic, one way is to shun any with swollen bases and white underneaths.

Perhaps the most widely known of the wild foods of the Far North is the lichen called rock tripe, whose growth reaches into the southern states. Rock tripe resembles a leathery dark lettuce leaf, up to about three inches wide, attached at its center to a rocky surface. Unless the day is wet, rock tripe is apt to be rather dry. It can be eaten raw, but you'll probably prefer it much of the time boiled to thicken soups and stews.

Reindeer moss, whose range also extends into the United States, is another edible lichen. It resembles moss, however, being a low greyish-green plant with a quantity of many-branched stems instead of leaves. Iceland moss, another edible lichen and not a moss, is found as far south as the States. Iceland moss is comparable to reindeer moss, being a brownish green plant whose numerous flat branches turn in to create a tube effect.

"Lichens are low, variously shaped, grey, brown, or black plants that are found throughout northern Canada and the

Arctic. They are edible," state Royal Canadian Mounted Police sources. "These lichens grow on both rocks and soil and are best collected when moist after rain. None of the lichens appearing in the Far North are poisonous, but most contain an acid that is bitter and sometimes nauseous and may cause severe internal irritation if not first extracted by boiling or soaking in water."

FIG. 20. Reindeer Moss.

A bitter lichen such as Iceland Moss is first boiled or soaked to remove this acrimoniousness. After being dried, it is powdered, perhaps by being rubbed between the palms. The resulting flour is sometimes used to stretch ordinary flour, and it is often utilized as is for making breadstuffs. The flour is also sometimes resoaked and finally reboiled to gruel-like and jelly-like consistencies which by themselves are short on taste but surpassingly long in nourishment.

Vegetarianism

"One farmer says to me," Thoreau recounted, 'You cannot live on vegetable food solely, for it furnishes nothing to make bones with'; walking all the while he talks behind his oxen, which, with vegetable-made bones, jerk him and his plow along."

Chapter 6

Go And Get It

FRESHLY CAUGHT FISH also provide a completely balanced diet when sufficiently fat and not overcooked. The main difficulty with subsisting exclusively on fish arises from the fact that in calories they are often far less nourishing than one might expect.

There are not many of us who will disagree it is with reason that rainbow trout are regarded as a delicacy hard to equal, nor that a rainbow weighing one pound when landed is a favorable size for the pan. Two or three such trout, most would be willing to concur, should afford the fisherman a reasonably substantial lunch.

Fateful Decision

Suppose there comes a time when you actually do have nothing to eat but trout? You're stranded in the wilderness, let us assume, about two days east of the Alaska Highway. No one knows you're missing, and therefore no one is searching for you. You know the general lay of the country well enough to be confident of cutting the Alaska Highway.

The area seems barren of game, but by really working at it you may reasonably expect to average catching a half dozen one-pound trout daily. Should you remain here a few days and live on fish, with the idea of building up your dwindling strength for the journey that still lies ahead?

An office worker undergoing very little physical exertion requires some 2000 to 2500 calories daily. It is reasonable to generalize that a man living a rugged outdoor life needs at least twice as many of these energy units. Any not supplied directly by food will be taken from the body's own carbohydrates, fats, and proteins.

A one-pound rainbow trout when caught, Canada's Department of National Health and Welfare has ascertained, contains only slightly more than 200 calories. So to eat some 4500 calories daily, you'd have to catch twenty such trout each day. Instead of gaining vigor on six pounds or so of fresh trout daily, you'd be very gravely losing strength. You'd do better to finish the journey as soon as possible.

Other considerations, of course, could alter the situation. You might have unlimited fish. You might be able to supplement the fish with sufficient other wild nutrient. The fish might be some more nourishing species such as, in some localities, fat salmon averaging closer to 900 calories per fresh raw pound.

Too, the wild food available might be yours so easily that you could conserve a decisive amount of energy by relaxing most of the time beside a warm blaze, for although the basal energy requirements of the human system decline but little even when one is starving, a man lounging comfortably before a campfire may consume only about 100 calories per hour, whereas struggling through the bush he can burn six times as much.

Wholesale Fishing With Bare Hands

Fish such as salmon and herring throng up streams in such numbers at certain times of the year that one can catch and throw ashore large numbers of them with the bare hands. It is also possible on occasion to secure by hand alone quantities of such fish as smelt, when schools come up on beaches to spawn in the surf.

Night Lines Work for You

A baited night line, affixed for its own protection to something limber such as the end of a sapling, is often productive when daytime fishing however arduous continues to be unsuccessful. Such a tactic in northern streams such as the Peace often yields the fresh-water cod known as the ling, an ancient species termed by some scientists a living fossil.

Those of us skinning and eating the uncomely ling for the first time are almost invariably surprised at the quality of its firm, rich savoriness. The vitamin-rich liver is widely esteemed, some cosmopolites considering it to be the greatest of all delicacies.

Sharks But Not Barracuda

Sharks are edible, although some may object to their taste. This can be notably improved if the meat is sectioned and then soaked in salt water for twenty-four hours. Barracuda, on the other hand, are sometimes poisonous.

All Seaweeds Edible

All seaweeds are good to eat. We munch them raw, simmer them in fresh water to make soup, boil them with meat and

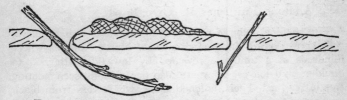

FIG. 21. It will often pay off to weave, twist, or knot together a gill net.

other vegetables, and even dry them for a number of other future uses. Algae, of which seaweeds are one type, are in fact regarded by research scientists as potentially valuable sources of the gigantic amounts of protein-rich food that may be needed if the increasing world population becomes so cumbersome that present supplies are inadequate.

Cucumbers That Are Alive

Sea cucumbers are eatable boiled, stewed, fried, and raw. Actually an animal, the sea cucumber is also dried and smoked by some natives. The easily recognizable organism, so common along seashores, has a rough and flexible body about six to eight inches long when contracted and about twice that length when expanded. The five long white muscles, which are left after the insides have been discarded and the slimy outer skin scraped away, are what is used. Their taste is not unlike that of clams.

All the Eggs You Want for Nothing

The sea urchin, a marine animal related to the starfish, is a principal source of nourishment in many localities. Safe when found in the temperate and arctic waters of this continent where they can be gathered in quantity at low tide, sea urchins are shaped like slightly flattened balls and have a thin fragile shell that bristles with movable spines. The lengths of eggs inside the top shell are edible both raw and cooked.

The Abalone Furnishes Its Own Bowl

The abalone, a large rock-clinging mollusk, is particularly well known along the Pacific coast of North America where hundreds at a time are revealed by low tides attached to boulders and ledges. They are also occasionally seen floating free in seaweed. Their flattened shells, which vary from black and green to red, are fantastically lined with mother-of-pearl.

By abruptly inserting a long thin instrument such as a sheath knife or stick between the abalone and the rock and prying quickly, the shellfish can be detached usually with little trouble before it has a chance to adhere more tightly. The operation otherwise requires a heavier tool and considerable pressure.

The abalone can then be levered from the shell, which not infrequently has a diameter of ten inches or so and therefore considerable utility as a bowl. Or the shell can be cracked with

FIG. 22. Sea cucumber.

a rock and picked off. The hard white meat is what is retained. This may be sliced into thin steaks and tenderized by pounding with the flat edge of a stone, then fried, broiled over open coals, or diced and simmered into chowder.

Other Free Lunches

Any time we may be up against it for food, there will be in general no more promising areas in which to seek nourishment than those near water. Piles of shells beside a creek may be the clue to clams that often can be seen in clear water or felt beneath the bare feet.

Salt water clams, although not so easily dug, may be secured at low tide, one indication of the bivalves' presence being their elongated siphons or the marks left by the withdrawals thereof. Along Pacific shores below the Aleutians, all dark portions should be discarded for the six months beginning with May and ending with October because of possibly dangerous concentrations of toxic alkaloids therein, the white meat alone then being eaten.

Snails are edible and by some peoples particularly relished. So are scallops, shrimps, and oysters. Eels are also esculent, in many localities being regarded as superior to any other fish.

Mussels, with one important exception, may be safely eaten

if care is taken to avoid any that do not close tightly when touched. The small bluish-black mussel found attached usually in clusters to seashore rocks becomes poisonous at certain times of the year along the Pacific coast below the Aleutians.

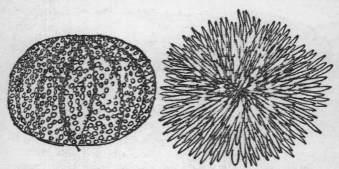

FIG. 23. Common Sea urchin, without and with spines.

The poison, which being an alkaloid cannot be destroyed by heat, is the result of a diet which includes venomous organisms that drift shoreward from about the end of April through October. If there is any doubt whatsoever about when in any particular area these mussels are fit for food, they should be avoided entirely.

Crabs are all good. They can usually be immobilized with a stick for a long enough time for one either to crush them or reach behind and pick them up. They will attach themselves readily to flesh lowered on a line. Although salt water varieties may be eaten raw, land crabs are sometimes infected with parasites and should be dropped into boiling water for at least twenty minutes.

What About Turtles?

Turtle fat, from which as you may have observed no more heat than that from the sun renders a clear savory oil, is so nutritious that the reptile is an unusually valuable food source Blood and juices are often used to relieve thirst.

It is sometimes possible to back track a female to a fresh nest of eggs, generally buried in sand or mud not far from water. Although not greatly esteemed for taste by those more accustomed to hen's eggs, these are nourishing in all stages.

The turtle can be killed by concussion or by decapitation, care being taken even after it is dead to avoid both jaws and

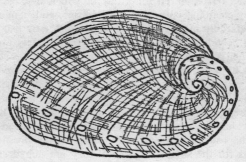

FIG. 24. Abalone.

claws. If it is convenient, the turtle can then be scalded for several minutes by being dropped into boiling water. The under shell may then be quartered and the entrails removed, whereupon the meat can readily be simmered free of the upper shell.

Cleaning Fish

Fish can be slit from vent to throat and the viscera removed easily and cleanly, in the case of pan fish often with a single stroke of the thumb. Many like to scrape away the blood vessels and kidneys which form dark lines next to the backbone. If the fish has scales, it can be held by the tail and these scraped off with the back of a knife or something similar.

You may not want to bother with head, tail, and fins of small fish except to eat around them, for bones will then hold together better and will not be so much of a nuisance. Furthermore, a few choice tidbits will be thus saved which would otherwise probably be wasted. If you ever have a number of heads, you may care to find out, perhaps by essaying a chowder with them, why these are regarded by many as the most delicious part of the fish.

Preserving Fish

Fish can be preserved for a day or two and longer by immediately cleaning, cutting into thin strips, and hanging these latter preferably in the wind and sun to dry. Any fish that are going to be retained should be killed immediately and, preferably, then kept dry.

If you have the time and want to keep fish for considerable periods, clean the fish, cut off the head, and then split each into two fillets so joined by the tail that they will hang over wooden racks. Build long fires beneath these racks. Keep the fires smoldering day and night with some green wood such as alder. The fish must be protected as much as possible from dampness for the several days until they are dehydrated.

Makeshift Fishing

Just because you don't happen to have a hook and line, that, as you very well realize, doesn't mean you can't catch fish. Unravel a bit of sweater, for instance. Tie on a small strip of bright cloth. The corner of a handkerchief will do. When the fish closes his mouth over the cloth, give the line a tug. There is a reasonable chance, especially where fishing is virgin, that you'll flip the quarry out on the bank. This doesn't always work, of course. Fish won't always take regular bait, either.

Hooks Made On the Spot

You can devise almost any number of different types of hooks. A bent pin really works, as many a youngster has learned, the only trick being to maintain pressure so that the fish won't slip off. An open safety pin is a somewhat larger hook of the same variety. Bent nails have been used with considerable success.

What follows, therefore, is that hooks can be made out of practically any workable metal of sufficient rigidity. If you want a really rugged one, lash the blade of a pocket knife partly open against a wooden wedge. A second blade, so opened at an opposite angle, can if available form a barb of sorts. The knife, so prepared, can then be hidden in a gob of bait.

You can also cut hooks from wood, preferably wood that is hard and tough. Whittle out the shank first. Lash one or more sharp slivers so that they slant upward from the lower end. You can even add a barb by lashing another sliver even more acutely downward from the top. Thorns if available can be utilized. Fish bones, too, will furnish both serviceable points and barbs.

Primitive Fishing Device

One of the most primitive fishing devices, still used successfully if not sportingly, is made by tying the line to the middle

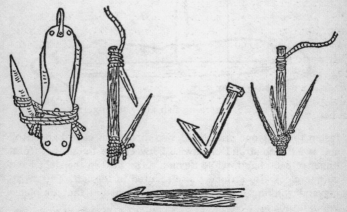

FIG. 25. Improvised fishhooks and a spear.

of a short piece of bone or wood that has been sharpened at each end. Hidden in bait, this is swallowed by the fish, whereupon a jerk of the cord pulls it crossways.

How to Make Fish Lines

Fish lines can be improvised in numerous ways. One method is to unravel a piece of fabric and to knot lengths of four or so threads together at frequent intervals. Another is to cut around and around a section of leather, forming a continuous lace.

Line can be more scientifically made, after cutting or raveling any fabric or fiber that may be available so as to procure a number of long strands. Take four of these threads and

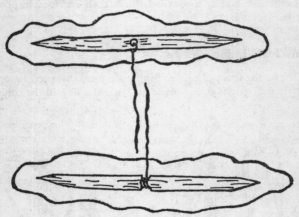

FIG. 26. Catching fish and scavengers.

fasten them at one end. Hold two threads in each hand. Roll and twist each strand clockwise between the thumb and forefinger of each hand, while turning those held in the right hand counterclockwise around those secured in the left. This twisting and winding must be done tautly, so that the completed line will not unravel.

Depending on the lengths of thread, conclude each of the

four strands about two inches apart so as to make the splicing on of fresh strands easier. About an inch before any thread stops, twist on a new strand to replace the one just ending.

This procedure can be continued, so long as materials hold out, to make a line of any length. The same operation that will provide a small cord for ordinary fishing can be employed with a dozen or more strands to manufacture a fish line capable of landing a tuna or big lake trout.

Buttons and Spoons

A button is often successful as a lure. So is any small bright bit of metal. In its emergency kit the Hudson's Bay Company, with characteristically commendatory frugality, includes a tablespoon with a hole drilled in it so that a hook can be wired in place for trolling or gigging.

Gigging So Deadly It's Illegal

Gigging, which is illegal in many localities and not without reason, is the practice of catching fish by hooking them anywhere in the body. An Eskimo method is to dangle a long smooth hook above which are suspended bits of bone that shine and flutter in the water. When a fish approaches to investigate, the line is suddenly jerked up the intervening two or three inches with a good chance of being driven into the prey which is at once hauled up before it has a chance to work loose. Gigging is often resorted to in waters where fish can be seen but not readily induced to bite.

Finding the Best Bait

Various insects, and even fuzzy seeds resembling these, will catch fish. Widely efficacious are grasshoppers, which when available can themselves be gathered with particular ease at night with the aid of a light.

"Experiment with bait," the Hudson's Bay Company advises any of its employees who may be in distress. "Look for bait in water, for this is the source of most fish food. Insects, crayfish, worms, wood grubs, minnows, and fish eggs are all good. After catching your first fish, examine the stomach and intestines. See what it was feeding on and try to duplicate it. If it is crayfish (form of fresh water crab), turn over the rocks in the stream until you get one."

If you succeed in finding many crayfish incidentally, there's your meal, for once they are cooked by being dropped into boiling water, the lower portion is easily sucked free of the shell. One way to catch these is by driving a school into a restricted pool and dipping them out with a net made either:

(1) by tightly interlacing foliage to a frame consisting of a bent green sapling,

(2) or by attaching some porous article of clothing to such a loop.

Getting Fish With Bare Hands

One spring vacation in the Berkshires, when I wasn't much older than ten, the fish at the bottom of a dam were biting so disinterestedly that I hid my rod and started wading around the boulders of the fast little river. I sloshed back that evening with a pretty good string of perch and trout after all. I'd found them wedged among the rocks.

Still another way to capture fish with the bare hands, I discovered later that same week, is by feeling carefully among the nooks and cavities in stream banks. You can even catch fish, strange to say, by forming a sort of cave with your cupped hands held motionless against a bank. Trout in particular will investigate, whereupon by the acquired art of closing the hands quickly enough but not too hurriedly you'll have them.

Emergency Measures That Procure Fish

When rations are short one can sometimes splash up shallow brooks, driving any fish ahead of him. When these are cornered in a pool, he can if he must block their retreat with piled stones and go in and kill them with a club. Small streams, too, can often be diverted so as to strand fish in pools.

If one is really up against it in beaver country, it is occasionally possible to strand a life-sustaining catch by prying an opening in a beaver dam. Another technique is to wade in, riling with the feet the muck that amasses behind such a dam and catching with bare hands the temporarily mud-blinded fish.

Making A Fish Trap

Fish can often be trapped with considerable success in cases of emergency. One such basic trap recommended by the Hudson's Bay Company for use under survival conditions can be made by driving sticks and branches into the bottom so

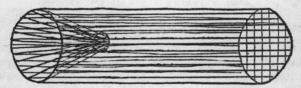

Fig. 27. Fish traps can be improvised from wire, vines, or branches.

that their tops protrude above the water. The trap, as the drawing shows, consists of a narrow-mouthed enclosure into which the fish are led by a wide funnel-like V.

Attracted by some such bait as spoiled fish or decomposed meat, the prey guided into the pen through the slit at the apex are in enough cases unable to find their way out.

Materials used in making such a trap vary. Stretching a net around stakes will, if the former is available, conserve considerable energy. Stones can be utilized, perhaps leading into a natural freshwater or tidal pool.

Spears and Spearing

You may have already experimented with making spears, perhaps sharpening a long dry stick for the purpose and hardening this point over the embers of a campfire. You've even fashioned a barbed spear possibly, whittling the point in this instance at the joint of an inverted crotch, an inch or two of whose angle you have slivered into a sharply restraining projection. You may have also tested the efficacy of barbs and tips of bone, metal, or stone that you have lashed into place.

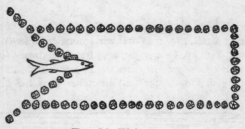

FIG. 28. Fish trap.

One procedure is to thrust the spear very slowly through the water toward the target, often to within inches of the fish before making the final jab. With the help of a light, possibly a torch of flaming birchbark or a burning pine knot, you can many times spot a fish at night lying practically motionless in shallow water. By advancing the spear cautiously, aiming low enough to counteract deceptive refraction, it becomes increasingly easy with practice to pin a majority of such fish against the bottom.

Drugging Fish With Local Vegetation

"Certain Indian methods of fishing may prove life savers for the hungry wayfarer," as noted in Vena's and my *How to Build Your Home in the Woods*. "One procedure is to crush the leaves and stalks of the mullein or fish weed, *croton setigerus*. These are dropped into a still pool or temporarily dammed brook. The fish therein, momentarily narcotized, will float to the surface where they should be immediately secured.

"The bulbous root of the so-called soap plant, *chlorogalum pomdeidianum*, can be similarly used. So can the seeds of the southern buckeye, *aesculus pavia*. Fish caught by these emergency means are as wholesome as if merely dazed by concussion."

Fig. 29 Spear.

Chapter 7

Always A Way

"YOU YAHOOS HAVE it too easy," it is the good-natured habit of Bill Carter, sourdough Peace River trapper, to grumble experimentally when the occasion promises to be productive. "When I joined the Mounted Police, all the equipment we got was a paper bag and a pointed stick. We used the bag to boil tea. The stick was for killing game. And if you lost either one, son, you got charged with it."

Outfitted with even less initial equipment one can actually exist very comfortably—with ingenuity, perseverance, and a fundamental understanding of how to go about it.

The Ideal Survival Weapon

Few who go into the matter will dispute that the ideal diet for the average individual stranded in the North American wilderness with inadequate food supplies is meat. Fat, rare meat will keep the human body supplied with all the vitamins, minerals, and other food substances necessary for the fullest enjoyment of peak health. Other wild foods will also accomplish this, but none in most instances as easily or as satisfactorily.

The challenge of survival will therefore in all likelihood be easier to meet if you have a firearm and ammunition. Suppose you have some choice in those two matters? Should you take a revolver, automatic pistol, shotgun, or rifle? What caliber? What type of ammunition?

You're considering the extreme problem of securing enough food to maintain strength indefinitely under primitive conditions, let us remember, perhaps for weeks and possibly for months without any outside help. The question viewed in that light becomes largely a matter of mathematics. What weight ammunition used with how heavy a firearm can reasonably be depended upon, pound for pound, to give you the most food?

Handguns, you will probably agree after following such reasoning a little farther, are not worth their weight and bulk as survival weapons if you have any choice in the matter. You can kill with them, certainly. The point is, because of inadequacies in such firearms themselves, no matter how expert you may be you cannot be reasonably sure of killing with them. You can hunt a month, even in ordinarily good country, and see only one moose. Your life can depend on your securing that one moose.

The best survival weapon, it follows, is a flat and hard shooting rifle. There is no need to append that it should be rugged, accurate, and durable. Neither is it necessary to add that a shotgun is no fit substitute, for although having about the same displacement and heft as a rifle, it shoots bulkier ammunition at much smaller prey.

Although it is true that something could be saved by procuring a carbine instead of a rifle, the extra weight and length would seem to be entirely justified by the increase in potential accuracy. As a matter of fact, it would be hard to begrudge the additional few ounces of a good telescopic sight if only because of the often vital minutes one adds to the most productive hunting periods of every day. You will probably want to include a light sling, such as a Whelen, if only for purposes of carrying.

As for ammunition, for several evident reasons, you'll want one shot to do the job whenever possible. You are therefore apt to prefer the explosive effect of a high velocity, hollow point cartridge.

Survival Weapons for Group

Suppose two or three of you each has an individual choice of survival weapons. Should one select a revolver, another a scatter gun, and the third the flat shooting and hard hitting rifle?

Some such diversification, at first thought, would not seem unreasonable. However, the same objections to handguns and shotguns would still prevail. You can see, upon consideration, that the probability of success would be greater if all had a rifle apiece, enabling you to spread out and hurt separately.

These rifles should all be identical, so that the parts of one or even two could be used to repair the third.

What and Where to Shoot

The first axiom of surviving by hunting, following the weight for weight formula to its inevitable conclusion, is to rely on big game. You will want to aim from the steadiest position possible for the vital region which affords the most margin for error, usually the chest.

Different Problems and Different Places

The fact that a variety of different types of firearms are included in the survival kits issued in quantity by various groups does not conflict with the preceding statements. Particularly as such outfits are made up en masse with the knowledge that only a very minor percentage of them will ever need to be used, qualifications such as expense and weight outweigh far more other considerations than they would otherwise.

The basic problem is different, however, in country such as the interior of Panama where there is abundant small game but little or no big game animals. In such a region a functional weapon for living off the country is a rifle for a load like the .22 Hornet. If one wanted to diversify his ammunition so as to be in a position to destroy a minimum of meat, he could also carry an amount of reduced loads having ballistics similar to those of the .22 long rifle cartridge.

The Extreme Importance of Glasses

Just the other afternoon I sat on a bluff, sunlight glinting into my eyes from the meandering Peace, and surveyed an open hillside a little more than a mile away. It seemed untenanted, and yet when I directed my Wollensak Mirroscope on it I could see a medium sized cinnamon bear gorging himself on saskatoons.

If I had needed meat, which I didn't, or wanted the glossy fur, which as a matter of fact I preferred to see on the bear, it would not in all likelihood have been too difficult to circle to within easy shooting distance. Yet although visibility was as good as could be expected where mountains rise in high wilderness as untouched as themselves, the berry bushes so camouflaged the bear that even knowing where he was I still couldn't make him out without the telescope.

The point is that when binoculars and other such glasses are fully capitalized upon, they are surpassed only by the firearm itself in importance in the matter of securing game vital for survival. If knocking down a meat animal can mean the difference between life and death, and particularly if your own life is not the only one so dependent, you're going to attempt a needlessly dramatic offhand shot. The same principle holds true in glassing the country for game. You'll find yourself holding the glasses as steadily as possible, utilizing any available support, sitting if you can, and even sprawling prone with the lenses resting on a log if afforded that opportunity.

An area, as one soon appreciates, is best scrutinized section by overlapped section. Any object that may conceivably be some part of an animal is patiently watched for minutes for any sign of movement. Even if none is distinguished, before shifting the field of vision you'll probably fix that particular spot in mind so as to study it later to see if any detail has changed.

You'll get the habit, likely as not, of carefully scanning game trails for as far as you can see them. You'll give particular notice to the types of cover where you know an animal may be lying and to the particular vegetation on which you are aware one may be feeding. Shores as everyone knows are especially well traveled, while in the water itself you too have perhaps more than once spotted moose dipping ungainly heads to uproot lily pads, and have spied bears and maybe even mountain goats swimming.

The Law of Survival

Few will not agree that practices ordinarily contrary both to game regulations and good sportsmanship are justified in extreme emergencies by the more ancient law of survival.

Under ordinary circumstances many of the methods of securing food herein deliberated are illegal practically everywhere and reasonably so, for a certain repugnance accompanies even the contemplation of some, while at best their successful commission in moments of stress will not be joined by any satisfaction except that resulting from the thus answered instinct to stay alive.

Jacking

One of these generally forbidden practices is jacking, in part the act of attracting and holding an animal's eyes at night by the beam of a light. Deer are among the big game creatures that can be readily spotted and held in this fashion long enough to be shot. Bear, on the other hand, will sometimes fall backwards in their haste to scramble out of the way.

Likely places for jacking are on the downwind sides of well used game trails and water holes. Licks are occasionally found where the ground is so tremulous that one may sleep in brush or tall grass until awakened by the quivering caused by the animal's weight. Strategically located trees are particularly favored locations, both because of the deceptive way one's scent is dissipated and because of the often increased visibility afforded by a seat high amid branches.

Procedure for any reasonable contingency should be well thought out ahead of time, for it will be necessary to move and hold the light so as to see both animal and sights. The darker the night is, as a matter of fact, the better in many respects it will be for jacking. During nights when the northern lights are bright or when the moon is large, on the other hand, one may be able to distinguish and shoot a game animal without additional illumination, particularly if he has a good light-gathering telescopic sight.

Suppose You Have No Gun

The Hudson's Bay Company recommends the use of deadfalls by any of its employees who may be stranded without adequate food in the northern wilderness where, some have claimed, man writes in vain a little history and nature buries it in a blizzard. The Company of Adventurers' pattern of the deadly Figure Four Trigger is here reproduced.

Essentially, you might prepare a deadfall by lifting one end of a heavy object such as a log. This end you would prop up with a stick, doing so with such studied insecurity that any animal or bird who moved the support would knock it loose. You would probably encourage this latter by affixing some bait to the prop. You might go even farther, arranging a few branches so that to reach the bait, the victim would place himself so as to receive the full weight of the dislodged deadfall back of the shoulders.

Making A Death Pit

If you may be in one place long enough to justify the effort, you might prepare a pit in a heavily traveled game trail and cover it as deceptively as possible with branches and leaves. Aborigines, to make sure that no animal will escape from such a hole, often implant sharpened sticks in the bottom of the trap to pierce anything that tumbles in.

Snares are Simple and Effective

Even if you do have a firearm, you may want to set a few snares, the principles of which are as simple as they are primitive. With a strong enough thong or rope, you can snare deer and larger animals. With nothing huskier than horsehair or light fish line, squirrels and rabbits can be caught.

FIG. 30. Deadly figure four trigger holding deadfall.

A snare is, in effect, a slip noose placed with the object of tightening about and holding a quarry if the latter inadvertently moves into it.

"The size of the snare depends on the size of the animal you are trapping," as the Hudson's Bay Company notes in the instructions it encloses in its own emergency kit. "For exam-

FIG. 31. Deadfall.

ple, on a rabbit trail the loop should be about four inches in diameter and hang from one-and-one-half inches to three inches above the ground."

Let us assume, for the sake of illustration, that we want to snare a rabbit for the pot. We can see that they, like other animals, follow regular paths. We will endeavor, therefore, to hang the slip noose so that the rabbit will run headfirst into it and quickly choke himself.

We may want to go one step further and narrow the trail at that particular spot. This we can accomplish in one of several ways. We can drop a branch or small tree as naturally as possible across the track, making a narrow slit in it in which to suspend the noose. We can shove a few sticks into the ground to serve as a funnel. We can block the bottom, top, and sides of the runway with brush except for a small opening where the loop awaits.

All possible guile will be bent to make everything seem as congruous as possible, an achievement whose necessity increases in direct proportion with the intelligence of the prey sought. Trappers customarily prepare snares months ahead and leave them, with the nooses harmlessly closed until fur season, to blend with the surroundings. Small pot animals, however, can usually be snared by beginners with a minimum of artifice.

FIG. 32. Bent-branch snare.   FIG. 33. Snare.

A quick way to collect squirrels, for instance, is to lean a pole against a conifer under which there is considerable squirrel sign and at six or so points on the pole attach small nooses. A squirrel scampering up the incline runs his head into the waiting loop and falls free. Its dangling there does not seriously deter other squirrels from using the same route and being so caught themselves.

We can tie one end of the snare to a stationary object such as a pole or tree. We can tie it, particularly if snow makes tracking easy, to a drag such as a chunk of deadwood. Preferably, as shown in the following illustrations of snares that have proved particularly effectual, we can bend a sapling and arrange a trigger so that the animal will be lifted off its feet and, if not choked as humanely as is possible under the conditions, at least rendered unable to exert direct pressure.

Besieging A Burrow

Distasteful as it may be to him, a starving man is occasionally forced to smoke small animals from places of concealment. Sometimes an animal can also be driven to within reach of a club by quantities of water being poured into a burrow.

The opening may be such that it will be possible to impale the creature on a barbed pole or to secure it by twisting a forked stick into its hair and skin. One is frequently able to dig with some success. One may also have some luck by spreading a noose in front of the hole, hiding a short distance away, and when the quarry ventures out jerking the loop tight.

Lemming for Emergency Diets

Lemming have been found valuable as an emergency food by members of the Royal Canadian Mounted Police on extended patrols. Lemming are the little stub-tailed mice that when reaching the ocean on their migrations, occasionally start swimming in the possible belief it is just another pond or lake.

"In winter they nest on or near the ground, deep in snowdrifts," say Mounted Police sources, "and you will have to dig for them. In summer, you can find them by overturning flat rocks. You can get them by setting snares of very fine wire along the runways. Lemming are constantly preyed upon by shrews, weasels, foxes, and owls."

These are edible, too.

Other Weapons

Both slingshots and bows and arrows are so familiar that, inasmuch as we will be limited in any event by the materials at hand, there will be no need to do more probably than to suggest them as survival weapons. As for their successful use, this will depend largely on individual practice. You will do the best you can and, if you have the ingenuity and resourcefulness necessary anyway for survival under extreme conditions, you are likely to do extremely well.

All Birds Are Eatable

All birds are good to eat. When they are molting and unable to fly, it is not difficult to corner them on foot. Large flocks may be occasionally captured by driving them into nets or traps. Roosting or nesting birds can be secured by a noose fastened to the end of a pole. Birds can also be caught in fine snares placed where they nest, feed, or congregate. Deadfalls immobilize them, too.

Even the riper eggs, or any eggs it may be possible to secure, are nourishing. If one has continued access to a large colony at nesting time, one way to be assured of fresh eggs is to mark whatever is already in the nests, perhaps removing all but a few if conditions seem to justify it.

Successful Bird Traps

Traps also work well with birds. A stick fence put up in a narrowing spiral and baited will sometimes catch, in its center, fowl such as quail. Geese can be bagged in a ditch some four feet deep into which they are led by bait such as wild grain. When one rushes suddenly at the geese, they try to fly but are unable to spread their wings.

Turkeys are also taken by the use of bait, one ruse consisting of attracting them head down under a low fence. Once turkeys so pen themselves and, upon finishing their pecking, raise their long necks, it often takes them too long a time to figure how to retreat.

Making And Using A Bola

One can improvise a bola, a missile weapon consisting primitively of stones attached to the ends of thongs. Although the Spanish people are generally most often thought of in connection with the bola, Eskimos use a device of this type consisting of several cords about a yard long with a small weight at the extremity of each.

The bola is grasped at the center from which all cords radiate, and the weights are twirled above the head. Twirled at flying birds, the spinning strings often twist around one or more and bring them to the ground.

Scavengers Easily Caught

Gulls and other scavenger birds can be easily although unpleasantly caught by a man who is desperate enough for food. A short stick or bone sharpened at both ends is secured in the middle by a line, preferably tied to something limber such as a sapling, and is then concealed in some bait such as a decomposed fish.

Mexican Stratagem With Numerous Possibilities

An ancient stratagem for capturing ducks, and one which can be varied almost indefinitely to fit the circumstances, had when Vena and I saw it enacted in old Mexico been set into motion by the tossing of dozens of gourds into a lake. The water fowl had become accustomed to them by the time a small dark native stole into the water, head hidden in a gourd which had been perforated to permit seeing and breathing.

The hunter advanced slowly toward a flock at about the same speed with which the shell might drift. Starting at the outside, he pulled ducks quickly downward by their feet, twisted their necks so we found out later, and shoved them one by one into a bag at his side.

Chapter 8

No Dishes To Wash

EVEN IF WE DON'T happen to have a frying pan along when on our own in the woods, the oversight need not necessarily be fatal. Actually the too often sanctified skillet is, particularly when loaded with grease, one of the deadlier weapons with which the wilderness is inflicted.

A few cooking utensils will make the job of preparing meals easier. Yet not only is none necessary, but the oftener the majority of us feast on such repasts as fat red sirloin that on a forked green stick has been broiled over the embers of a campfire, the more such primitive methods of cookery continue to please.

Tidbits of meat skewered on a green wand, thrust briefly into licking flames to seal in the juices, and then cooked not too near the steady heat of glowing coals—with the deliberateness as necessary for proper anticipation as for rightful succulence—have been a favorite noonday repast of some of us for years. You may be numbered among those who like to gnaw each bite-size morsel off the stick as wanted, returning the spit to the warmth in between times so as to keep any remaining kabobs sizzling.

Broiling on a Stick

A fish, bird, or small animal may be cleaned and then impaled in whatever way may be most convenient on a green hardwood stick. The top of the stick itself can as a matter of fact be split and, reinforced if necessary at either or both ends of the cleft by its own twisted and tied bark, clamped over the food. Many of us find it preferable to sear meat by shoving it momentarily into the blaze and then to hold it over a bed of embers, scraping a few to one side of the fire if flames are still lifting ardently. For the prime secret of such campfire cookery is, if it is to be most successful, to cook unhurriedly with the uniform hotness of hardwood coals.

If we've other matters to attend to before eating, we can lay the spit between two crotched uprights, prop it over a stone, or merely push one end into the ground, thereafter pausing only to examine and occasionally to turn the meat until the meal is ready.

Baking on a Stick

Baking on a stick is so handy, especially when we're preparing only small amounts to be eaten hot, that you may already be in the habit of preparing bannock in this fashion while kabobs are sputtering, having carried the dry ingredients ready mixed so that nothing remained but to add enough water to make a stiff dough.

The basic recipe for this backwoods bread consists of one cup of flour, one teaspoon of baking powder, and one-fourth teaspoon of salt. To this may be added, depending on tastes and availabilities, a variety of spices and fruits as well as sugar and one or another shortening.

You'll be heating a peeled green stick of hardwood, which may be about as thick as the forearm of a hunting rifle. The dough you will mold swiftly, so as not to lose too much of the carbon dioxide gas whose function it is to make the breadstuff rise, quickly fashioning a wide ribbon to twist around the stick. A few stubs on the latter, left by not trimming it too smoothly, will help keep the soft mass in place during the baking.

Cooking on Individual Plates

Fish can be pegged on preheated hardwood slabs and leaned
before a bank of glowing coals. If after they are opened and
cleaned there is any difficulty in making them lie reasonably
flat with their skin against the wood, the backbone may be
removed. Turning the slab a time or two will give the flesh
a better opportunity to become flaky throughout.

The reason for recommending hardwood in these instances
is well understood. particularly by those who have learned by
experience how the pines and other evergreens can flavor food
strongly enough to hide the often preferable natural taste.

The motive for specifying green wood is equally evident.
The wet green hardwood that grows beside streams is in
general a particularly functional choice, being even less prone
to burn. Birch does burn readily when green, although the
slight amount of extra care thus necessitated is more than
rewarded in this instance by the impartation of a delicately
sweet aroma.

Such a slab, and a flat rock as well, can also be heated and
used like a hot plate.

Steaming in Hole

The hole is most easily scooped out of sand. A fire should
already be blazing and in it heating a few stones, care being
taken that these are not of the stream bed variety which may
contain water that, turning to steam, can cause a perhaps
dangerous explosion.

Shove the hot stones into the hole, press a thick layer of
some wet green growth such as seaweed or damp grass over
them, lay on the food, add an upper sheathing of similar
damp vegetation, and then fill in the rest of the cavity with
sand or loam. Open enough of an inlet with a stick to allow
some additional water to be poured on the rocks, and then
stamp the topping down compactly.

The food can then be safely left to steam until you're ready
for it, the length of the cooking process depending as might
be expected on a number of variables but usually requiring at
least several hours.

Baking in Clay

What amounts to small individual ovens can be provided by covering a fish, bird, or small animal with stiff moist clay about an inch thick. This clay may be worked into a sheet on the ground and then shaped around the food like dough, or the article may be dipped and redipped as often as necessary in a thinner mixture.

Most of us will probably want to remove entrails first, but no scaling, plucking, or skinning should be done, for this will be accomplished in a single operation when we break open and strip off the hard adobe made by laying the whole thing in hot ashes above which a fire is burning.

Time required for cooking will vary according to individual taste. A half-hour beneath ashes and embers readies a one-pound rainbow to my own personal satisfaction, but very understandably you may like trout cooked more or possibly even less. At any rate, when done it will be ready to serve with all the juices sealed in, an often pleasant relief after the dryness unnecessarily associated with so much outdoor cookery.

Oven in Clay Bank

If the chances are that we will be in one place long enough to merit the effort, we may elect to make an oven in a clay slope or bank. One way to commence this is by hammering a sharpened pole, about as thick as the forearm, straight down into the bank about three feet back from the edge.

Then a foot or so down the side of the bank, far enough to allow a sturdy ceiling, let us scoop out the size oven we want. A usual procedure is to shape it like a beehive, with a narrow entrance. We will dig back as far as the pole, of course, which we'll then pull out to form the chimney. We can give the interior a hard coating by smoothing and resmoothing it with wet hands. A small blaze may then be kindled within to harden this lining.

It is very possible that we will be able to find an old burrow to serve as the basis for such a contrivance. Or, at the other extreme, we can do as I have in New Mexico: construct a rough form of arched green sticks and daub the wet clay in thick layers over this. These successive layers may be allowed to dry in the sun, or each succeeding process can be quickened by small fires lit within.

Baking in such an oven is simplicity itself. The oven is pre-heated by a fire kindled inside. Fire and ashes are then scraped out. The food is laid within on stones, or leaves, or whatever may be handy. Both flue and front opening are tightly closed. One then goes about his business. The meal will cook without further attention.

Cooking in Ashes

The majority of us have at one time or another roasted veg-etables in the ashes of a campfire, perhaps merely dropping or shoving them out of sight or, more scientifically, baring a heated bit of ground where the vegetables could be de-posited and warm ashes and finally embers pushed over them. Timing is, as with most such cooking, a matter of some ex-perimentation.

Not so many have also baked breadstuffs in this latter fash-ion, with surprising cleanliness incidentally, first rolling them a little more heavily than usual in flour. When we remember that the white of hardwood ashes can be substituted in equal quantities for baking soda in preparing dough, this practice may not seem so unusual.

Barbeque

Anyone having sufficient fat meat to warrant the sacrifice of some nutriment in exchange for the psychological stimulus of a barbeque may want to allow a hardwood blaze to crum-ble to embers in a pit, over which green poles can then be spread and slabs of meat lain.

These chunks should be turned after a minute or two to sear in the juices, which will be further guarded if during subsequent handling the meat is not cut or pierced. The flavor will be the better if any flames that lick up from time to time, particularly when grease begins to drop, are immediately quelled.

Containers

Suppose we're without cooking implements and want to heat a liquid. Some large shells may be lying about, or perhaps we can find a stone with a hollow in it. If the stone is small enough, let us build a fire around it. If it is too ponderous for that, then why not preheat it by lighting the conflagration in the cavity itself?

We can fold a large rectangle of moist birchbark inward at each of its four corners and hold the resulting receptacle in shape with wooden skewers. A long wide strip of bark can also be folded in at the two ends to make a container shaped outwardly like a split log. A round piece of bark, first soaked if necessary to render it sufficiently pliable, can be tucked in once to provide a conical cup.

It is usually a matter of some wonderment, when we try it first, to find that water can actually be boiled in something as unpretentious as birchbark if flames are kept from touching this above the water level. It is also easy enough to drop some clean pebbles into a large inflammable container and then add hot stones from a campfire, handling them with tongs made by bending a limber green stick.

Making a Soup Hole

You've just killed a moose. Hungry, you've a hankering for nothing quite as much as some hot soup, flavored perhaps with wild leeks whose flat leaves you see wavering nearby. Why not take the sharp end of a dead limb and scoop a small hole in the ground? Why not line this concavity with a chunk of fresh hide? Then after adding the water and other ingredients, why not let a few hot clean stones do your cooking while you finish dressing out the animal?

FIG. 34. Wild Onion.

Butchering

Butchering as we know offers no particular problems to anyone with a sharp knife. If without a knife, as sometimes happens, we can only do the best we can, puncturing and tearing more than cutting, and improvising as well as possible with a thin-edged rock or the jagged end of a dead limb.

Birds, we learn, can be dressed in a few moments with the bare hands alone. The feathers can be pulled out with the least damage to the succulent skin when the fowl is still warm. If we have more birds than time, we may strip off skin and feathers in one smooth operation.

If we see a small pouch near where the neck disappears into the body, we pull that off, perhaps examining it to see what the species is eating, for it is the crop. Then we pull the bird open, grasping it above and below the ribs. When we take out the viscera thus revealed, most of us will save the heart and liver. The gizzard is good, too, once it has been opened and emptied.

Food animals, experience teaches us, are often most easily skinned when hung by the separated hind legs. We cut around each ankle. We slit up the inside of the leg to join a long cut made from the vent up the abdomen of the animal to the throat. We do the same with each foreleg. Then we pull down the skin, using the cutting edge whenever it becomes necessary to free the hide from the body.

Animals are carefully opened from vent up through the ribs and all the innards pulled out with as little cutting and puncturing as possible. Liver, kidneys, and heart are the parts most often saved. The flavor of small creatures such as muskrats is improved when care is taken to cut out the stringy white scent glands from the insides of the forelegs and thighs.

How to best Blowflies

Meat can be protected from the big-egg-laying blowflies by keeping it in a dark cold place such as a dry cave, by hanging it clear of foliage upwards of four yards above the ground, and to some extent by suspending fresh chunks in the smoke of a small fire until a protective casing hardens around them.

Preserving Meat by Drying

One of the easiest primitive ways to preserve meat is by drying. This we can do by cutting it into long thin strips and hanging them apart in the sun, whereupon they will eventually lose most of their water content and become dry, hard, black, and incidentally both sustaining and delicious.

The strips can be soaked first, if one desires, either in brine or sea water. One method is to boil down ocean water until it becomes extremely salty and, while it is still simmering, to dip the strips in this. If there is no place handy to hang the meat, it can be laid on sun-heated rocks and turned every hour or so.

The process that Colonel Townsend Whelen describes may become your favorite as it has mine.

"Jerky is lean meat cut in strips and dried over a fire or in the sun. Cut the lean, fresh red meat in long wide strips about half an inch thick. Hang these on a wood framework about four to six feet off the ground. Under the rack, build a small, slow, smoky fire of any nonresinous wood. Let the meat dry in the sun and wind. Cover it at night or in rain. It should dry in several days.

"The fire should not be hot enough to cook the meat at all, its chief use being in keeping flies away from it. When jerked, the meat will be hard and more or less black outside, and will keep almost indefinitely away from damp and flies.

"It is best eaten just as it is; just bite off a chunk and chew. Eaten thus, it is quite tasty. It may also be cooked in stews. It is very concentrated and nourishing, and a little goes a long way as an emergency ration, but alone it is not a good food for long-continued consumption, as it lacks the necessary fat."

The fat, which would turn rancid, should be trimmed off before the drying operation is commenced. A conservative procedure is to render it, either for later use as a food supplement or for more immediate employment in the manufacture of pemmican.

Pemmican

"To make pemmican you start with jerky and shred it by pounding," suggests Colonel Townsend Whelen. "Then take a lot of raw animal fat, cut it into small pieces about the size of walnuts, and try these out in a pan over a slow fire, not letting the grease boil up. When the grease is all out of the lumps, discard these and pour the hot fat over the shredded jerky, mixing the two together until you have about the consistency of ordinary sausage. Then pack the pemmican in waterproof bags. The Indians used skin bags."

The ideal proportions of lean and fat in pemmican is by weight approximately one-half well dried lean meat and one-half rendered fat. It takes about five pounds of fresh lean meat to make one pound of dried meat suitable for pemmican.

Such true pemmican, extremely seldom obtainable commercially, will afford practically every necessary food element with the exception of Vitamin C. This you can probably get along without for at least two months, however, if already in good health. Supplementing this pemmican with fresh food will, on the other hand, supply the Vitamin C necessary to prevent scurvy.

Chapter 9

Thirst

WHEN WOOD smoke lifts among spruce in patterns as primitive as those formed there other days by frost crystals, have you sometimes found yourself wishing you could taste peace and quiet and solitude long enough to find out how good they—and you—really are?

Maybe you've even put into words this natural yearning of that portion of our most primitive ancestor which survives within us. You've added perhaps that circumstances may conceivably be such for anybody, whether because of misadventure or storm or man-loosed disaster, that tomorrow he will be alone in the wilderness and compelled to rely solely on his own ingenuity and resourcefulness for survival.

What is the first doubt that besets most individuals at such a suggestion but the worry that, if forced to shift for themselves in the unfrequented Farther Places, they would starve?

The truth of the matter is, as we have learned, that a healthy human being can get along entirely without food for a month or two under favorable conditions. Anyone would do well to stay alive for much more than a week if he did not have water.

There fortunately need not often be a shortage of drinking water, especially when we understand how to locate some of the more unusual sources now recognized by only a very few. The much more common problem lies in making sure that water so come upon is fit for human use. Comprehending a minimum of fundamentals, this we can also solve with reassuring certainty, for it is only the most basic common sense never to take the slightest unnecessary risk with doubtful water.

Any of us can generally get along a while longer without a drink. Just moistening our lips in water one drop of which is contaminated can, on the other hand, so sicken us that if nothing worse we'll become too weak to travel.

The Safest Principle Regarding Purity

How can we tell then if water is pure? Short of laboratory tests we can not, for even where a mountain rill bubbles through sheer mountain fastnesses, the putrifying carcass of a winter-killed animal may be lying a few yards upstream.

The folklore that any water a dog will drink is pure enough for his master is unfortunately as baseless as it is charming, as even the fondest owner must testify upon recalling a few of the potions his pet has assimilated with impunity. The more reasonable assumption that anything your horse will drink is safe for humans is likewise at fault, inasmuch as pollution may be entirely odorless, whereas an equine's basis for rejection or acceptance is familiarity of smell.

The fact that natives may assert a water source is pure may mean, instead, that either they have built up a certain degree of immunity or that because of familiarity they can not believe the water is tainted. A domestic water supply used by the inhabitants and guests of a Montana ranch for some twenty years was found to have been infecting not only present but previous users with tularemia, the germs of which can be carried to water by pets such as dogs and domestic beasts such as pigs even though they themselves may seem perfectly healthy.

Even the loneliest wild stream can be infected with this so-called rabbit fever by such wild animals as muskrats and beavers. Yet taking a chance with drinking water in a well-settled community is in one sense a lot less dangerous than laying ourselves open to a small fraction of similar risk in wilderness where medical help may be hours and perhaps weeks away. The safest principle in any event is to assume all water is impure until it has been proved otherwise, positively and recently.

Making Sure it's Pure

Water can be rid of germs by boiling. The exact time required to accomplish this depends on altitude, the nature of any impurity, and several other factors that altogether are so elastic that although a shorter time will often suffice, a safe general rule is to boil questionable water at least five minutes.

If there is any reasonable doubt that water may be contaminated, it would be hard for the most hurried and harried of us not to agree that it should be purified before human use although such a process may be expected to require both time and trouble. A great deal more inconvenience and delay can result from using just any water indiscriminately.

Nor does this apply only to water that is actually drunk. It is applicable with equal gravity to any water a drop of which may enter the human body; examples being, as may be appreciated, water in which the toothbrush is dipped, water in which food utensils are washed, and water used in cooking except when kept at a high enough temperature for a sufficient time to insure purity.

Boiled water, as everyone knows, tastes flat because air has been driven from it by heat. Air and therefore taste can be restored by pouring the cooled water back and forth between two utensils or by shaking it in a partially filled jar or canteen. Or if one is in a hurry and has salt, it is a common practice to add a pinch of that.

Simple Chemical Purification

One can purchase at most sporting goods and drugs stores for about fifty cents a small two-ounce bottle containing one hundred halazone tablets. Since their purifying action depends upon the release at the proper time of chlorine gas, these should be fresh and the container kept tightly closed and its contents dry.

No purification of water by chemical means is as dependable as boiling, but two halazone pills will ordinarily make a quart of water safe for human consumption in a half-hour. If the water is muddy or if its integrity seems particularly questionable, it is good insurance to double at least the amount of halazone and preferably the time as well.

Care should be taken with chemical purifiers so employed to disinfect all points of contact with the container, so that the water once sterilized will not be easily reinfected. If a jar or canteen is being used together with halazone, replace the cover loosely and wait two or three minutes so that the tablets can dissolve. Then shake the contents thoroughly, allowing some of the fluid to spill out over the top and lips of the holder. Tighten the cover then and leave it that way for the desired time before using any of the liquid.

You Can Use Chloride of Lime

Chlorine in some form is regarded as the most dependable disinfectant for drinking water. When introduced in proper quantities it destroys any existing organisms, and for as long as enough remains in the water it prevents recurring contamination. It is better to err moderately on the side of overdosage if at all, for waters of varying chemical and physical composition react differently to equal quantities of a given disinfectant, just as two individuals are to some degree diversely affected by like doses of an antibiotic.

Emergency chlorination of drinking water may be accomplished in three steps:

(1) dissolving one heaping tablespoon of chloride of lime in eight quarts of water,

(2) adding one part of this solution to one hundred parts of the water to be disinfected,

(3) and waiting at least thirty minutes before using.

The stock solution should be kept tightly corked in preferably a cool, dark place, and even then it should be frequently renewed.

Iodine as a Germicide

Tincture of iodine can be used as an emergency water purifier. A drop of this fresh antiseptic, mixed thoroughly with one quart of water in the same manner as halazone, will generally make the water fit for human consumption in thirty minutes. Both the amount and the time may be doubled if this precaution seems warranted.

Iodine Water Purification Tablets

Chlorine-releasing compounds can not be relied upon in semi-tropical and tropical areas. Neither there nor anywhere else, incidentally, does the addition of liquor to water or ice rid either of the latter of germs. Water in these aforesaid regions should be boiled or when this is not feasible treated with Iodine Water Purication Tablets. Containing the active Tetraglycine Hydroperiodide, these have been adopted as standard for the armed services of the United States.

The tablets have been proved effective against all the common water-borne bacteria as well as the Cysts of Endamoeba Histolytica and the Cercariae of Schistosomiasis. Manufactured by the Maltbie Laboratories Division of Wallace & Tiernan, Inc. of Belleville, New Jersey, fifty tablets are packaged in a glass bottle with a wax sealed cap. Each tablet, 7/32 of an inch in diameter, weights approximately 120 milligrams. Added to water, each tablet frees eight milligrams of iodine which acts as a water purification factor. One tablet will purify one quart of water.

These tablets, too, must be kept dry. The bottle, therefore, should be recapped tightly after being opened. Directions for use are:

(1) add one tablet to quart of water in container with cap,

(2) wait three minutes,

(3) shake water thoroughly, allowing a little water to leak out and disinfect the screw threads before tightening container cap,

(4) wait ten minutes before drinking or adding beverage powders, and if water is very cold, wait twenty minutes,

(5) if water contains decaying vegetation or is murky and discolored, use two tablets for every one quart,

(6) make certain that the iodine disinfects any part of the container which will come in contact with the drinker's lips.

How to Recognize Poisonous Water Holes

A few water holes, as in the southwestern deserts of this continent, contain dissolved poisons such as arsenic. One is usually able to recognize such a water hole easily, partly because bones of unwary animals may be scattered about, but mainly because green vegetation will be conspicuously absent. The safest general rule, therefore, is to avoid any water holes around which green plants are not thriving.

Hard Water

If in the section where we may be traveling there is hard water to which we are not accustomed, severe digestive upsets may result if while getting used to it we sip more than small amounts at any one time. Boiling may be of some help, inasmuch as when magnesia and lime carbonates are held in solution by carbon dioxide, these hardening agents can be partially solidified by the driving off of the gas by heat.

How to Make a Filter

Water can be cleared by filtration, although this process will neither materially affect any dissolved minerals, nor will it assure purity. Water is polluted by animal and mineral matter, rather than by discoloring vegetable substances such as grass roots and dead leaves. The first two can not be removed with any sureness by ordinary filtering.

The function of the makeshift filter is to clear water by straining solid materials from it. You may be canoeing up near the Yukon border on the Sikanni, for example, which is so muddy that some rivermen save time and effort by lugging kegs of drinking water with them. Filtration will serve instead, however.

A wilderness filter can generally be made without too much trouble, particularly in sand, by scooping a hole a few feet from the source of supply and using what water seeps into it.

A Way to Sweeten Water

One evening we may make camp in a swamp or by a pond which has an unpleasant odor. It will be handy in such a contingency to know how to sweeten and purify water in a single operation.

This we can usually accomplish by dropping several bits of charred hardwood from the campfire into the boiling pot. Fifteen or twenty minutes of simmering will usually do the job. One of us can then skim away most of the foreign matter, and then either strain the water by pouring it through a clean cloth or, if we've plenty of time and utensils, merely allow it to settle.

Where to Find Water

One is always learning from nature, if indeed he will learn at all, and not the least pleasurable of these gifts is the widening ability to determine with little if any conscious effort where water lies in a wilderness area. Several principles serve to aid one in this discernment, and these everyone knows already: that water flows downhill, that it grooves the face of the world while so doing, and finally that it encourages vegetation and particularly some types of vegetation.

We are not surprised in high country to find water near the tops of mountains, perhaps indicated by a comparatively lush area or, sometimes, by a thread of green verdancy unraveling down a slope. Perhaps, too, a glacier or permanent snowbank may furnish refreshment.

Water is also prone to lie near the base of hills, where it can many times be distinguished in distant ravines and canyons by the intensity of vegetation. The main problem, as a matter of fact, often becomes less the discovery of water than the finding of a sufficiently gradual descent to it.

When country is flat and open, long meandering tangles of such brush and shrubs as alder and willow tell us all their familiar story.

When to Follow Game Trails

Game trails very often indicate the presence of water, a

usually reliable indication being a marked increase and a progressive deepening and widening thereof. If we want water, what we will do of course is follow these.

If however we are traveling in the north with the object of making time, we will come to recognize that such trails commonly mean a muskeg lies ahead and that the easiest procedure will very possibly be the following of the animal thoroughfares around it.

Locating Water on a Seacoast

One often successful procedure for locating drinking water on an ocean beach is to wait until low tide and then dig below the high water mark. There will generally be some object such as a shell available that can either be used by itself as a scoop or lashed to a length of driftwood to provide a shovel. Fresh water, if there is any, will remain atop salt water because it is lighter. The hole for that reason should not be deepened beneath the first signs of seepage, at least not until a reasonable water supply is assured.

Desert Water

Water seeks the lowest levels available, and on the desert these may be underground. If there seems to be no particular direction in which you should travel and you can see hills, head toward them, for the likeliest place to locate water will be at their base.

Perhaps you'll come across the thin shallow bed of a stream. Even though it is dry, water may lie beneath the surface. Hunt for a low place in the cut and dig. The same procedure may be followed in the case of dry lake bottoms. The presence of any water will soon be indicated by damp sand.

Game trails in desert country usually lead to water. Follow them downhill if the land so slopes that you can do this with certainty. Otherwise, scout until you can make sure in which direction the paths have become more frequented, and this will be the way to go.

If you happen upon a palm, you can depend on water being

at hand, generally within several feet of the base of the tree. Reed grass is also a sound sign that moisture is near.

Rain Water

When up against it for water, it is sometimes possible to find rain that has accumulated in the large leaves of plants and trees or that has been trapped in natural basins such as are frequent in rocky terrain.

Moisture From Vegetation

Discovering water in vegetation is most spectacular in desert regions, where the various cacti are able to thrive because of an ability to store fluid in the form of thin watery sap which, in turn, can furnish a human being with an emergency drink.

If you need that juice, you'll cut off sections of cactus and, being continually wary of spines, mash them in a container. You'll either drink any resulting fluid on the spot or pour it into a second container, and then you will repeat the process as often as necessary or expedient. If you have no utensils, you'll mash segments of the cactus one by one and suck the pulp.

Some of the larger cacti such as the barrel cactus, which looks about like what might be expected from the name, will provide their own utensils. The top can be sliced off if necessary, the soft interior crushed to pulp, and the watery sap either scooped out with the cupped hand or imbibed from a hole tapped in the side.

Snow

Clean snow may be eaten any time one is thirsty. The only precaution that ever need be taken is to treat it like ice cream and not put down too much at once when overheated or chilled. One of the pleasantest wilderness desserts, as a matter of fact, is ice cream made with snow. You just pour milk into a container, add sugar and some flavor such as chocolate, and stir in preferably fresh light snow until taste and texture are satisfactory.

Snow, after all, is in flake form the purest of distilled water obtainable from the atmosphere. Its only drawback is that a considerable amount is required to equal a glass of water. One soon learns to break off sections of crust when this is available. Heavy granular snow from former storms is usually better yet. Most concentrated, of course, is ice itself.

One finds out about low water content very quickly when melting snow in the noon tea pail. Particular care has to be taken not to burn the pot, first of all, the best procedure being to melt snow in small quantities until the bottom of the utensil is safely covered with several inches of water. Secondly, the container must be filled with more snow and refilled probably a time or two more if anything like a capacity amount of liquid is desired.

This nuisance is compensated for by the fact that snowfall makes water readily available throughout the wilderness. All one has to do is scoop up clean handfuls while walking along, a valuable convenience inasmuch as one requires a lot more water in cold weather than he'd ordinarily expect, the kidneys then having to take over much of the process of elimination otherwise accomplished by the sweat glands.

Ice

The winter water supply of many an Arctic establishment consists of what is adjudged to be a sufficient number of blocks of laboriously procured ice. The task of melting these is sufficiently inconvenient, however, that when it is feasible most prefer to chop or chisel water holes in lake or stream ice. Such holes may be kept covered to discourage their refreezing.

As far as purity is concerned, ice and the water obtained from melting ice differ in no respect from the water originally frozen. Although heat kills germs, cold does not.

With the danger of germ warfare not becoming less in this civilization, it is at least indicative of what we may be up against to review the following facts:

(a) thousands died from an especially virulent contagion of influenza that followed World War I,

(b) recently bacteriologists wanting to study the flu organisms journeyed to the Arctic to disinter Eskimos who had died during that epidemic,

(c) the scientists thought they might be able to secure live cultures from the cadavers which had been buried in the cold regions for more than a quarter of a century,

(d) they were successful.

Salt Water Ice Becomes Fresh

"The soundest reasoning leads to the wrongest conclusions when the premises are false," as Dr. Vilhjalmur Stefansson points out. "There are few things considered more certain than that the ocean is salt, and there is no inference more logical (although no inference is ever really logical) than that the ice of salt water must also be salt."

It so happens, notes Stefansson who is often called the greatest living explorer, that sea ice becomes fresh during the period intervening between its formation and the end of the first summer thereafter.

If during freezing weather you are ever in a position where you have no other source of water but salt water, as a matter of fact, you will want to catch small amounts of the available brine and allow ice to form in it. The slush and any remaining liquid should then be removed. The ice you'll find fresh enough to use in the emergency.

Ocean ice loses its salt so rapidly that ice one year old is nearly fresh, and ice formed two or more years before can not be distinguished as far as taste goes from river ice unless waves have been breaking over it recently or spray has been dousing it. Melted hollows, otherwise, will usually be found to contain ample fresh water.

Finding Drinking Water on Ocean

Rain will often furnish drinking water at sea if, when it starts to fall, the precaution is immediately taken to let it wash any accumulated salt from everything that is to be used for catching and storing it.

Dew is heavy enough in some localities to merit being caught in a sail or tarpaulin stretched with sufficient sag to allow any condensation to collect.

One may be out of sight of land and yet so near the mouth of some great river that even far at sea the water will still be fresh. If such may be the case, it may not be a profitless procedure to test the water from time to time by touching the tongue to a moistened finger.

"If all other means of obtaining drinking water have been exhausted, any metal container and lighted lantern may be used to obtain water by condensation," suggests the United States Air Force. "Remove one end of the container and submerge the closed end in a foot or more of salt water. Place the lighted lantern inside the container, on the bottom. Cover the open top, allowing only enough air to enter to keep the lantern burning. The heat will cause moisture to form on the inside of the container. This can be soaked up with a rag and squeezed into a cup."

Obtaining Water From Fish

The proportion of water in fish runs so particularly high that at sea, except when large enough emergency water supplies can be secured from ice or rain, fish are the most dependable source. These can be caught in numerous different ways, many of which we have already considered in Chapter 6. In some waters a plenitude of fish will even leap freely aboard at night, especially if a light is shown to attract them.

Most sea life can be used, although crabs and sharks are excessively salty unless there is ample fresh water. Sea snakes, which unlike eels have no scales, are edible but have poisonous fangs. Unless the fish you catch has ordinary scales and looks like most fish you are accustomed to seeing, a good rule especially in warm waters is to leave it alone. Jellyfish should neither be handled nor used. Even the very tiny ones are disagreeably bitter.

Water can be obtained from freshly caught fish in several different ways. The most fundamental method is to divide the flesh into small portions and to chew each of these thoroughly, expectorating all solid matter before going on to the next morsel. The fish can also be sectioned and twisted within a cloth, the thus freed juice either being sucked up or caught. One primitive way of dealing with a large fish is to hack holes in its sides and allow moisture from the lymphatic vessels to ooze into these.

If you like the juice of raw clams and oysters, you're apt to find all this surprisingly pleasant. At any rate, you'll thus be able to satisfy thirst for as long as you can catch sufficient fish.

Quenching Thirst at Sea

The blood from any birds you can secure will help quench thirst. So will the blood of turtles. If drinking water is lacking, the flesh of both can also be chewed until all moisture is extracted, and then expelled.

Salt Water

One characteristic of salt water making it totally unfit for use as drinking water is its cathartic property. An example of this, occasionally capitalized on in the backwoods, is that a quart of warm water in which a rounded teaspoon of table salt has been dissolved will ordinarily pass through the digestive system in about half an hour if taken on an empty stomach upon rising.

When there is a scarcity of fresh drinking water, every effort should usually be made to discourage anyone's drinking salt water, for this will not only give rise to tormenting thirst in part by diminishing moisture already in the body, but it will progressively weaken one, cause actual poisoning, and if continued without relief inflict eventual madness.

Salt Intake in Hot Weather

There is a time, however, when the drinking of some salt water is to be recommended. On hot days when the normal supply of salt in the human body is depleted by perspiration and when no amount of fresh liquids will seem to sate the thirst, what the system often needs is salt. This can be supplied by making every cup of drinking water from one-fifth to two-fifths sea water, or by adding a salt tablet or one-fourth teaspoon of table salt to each cup of fresh water.

Other Things to Avoid When Thirsty

When one becomes extremely thirsty, any liquid is a temptation. If you should ever be in such a plight, you'll want to warn any companions against drinking alcoholic beverages which, aside from other possibly dangerous effects, will only further dehydrate the body.

Medicines, it will be realized, cannot be substituted for drinking water either. Most compass fluids are poisonous antifreezes. Body wastes contain harmful by-products and at best will only increase thirst. Smoking, incidentally, is dehydrating and heightens the need for fluid.

Sluggishness of the digestive system is a natural consequence of going without normal amounts of water and nourishment. This condition need not cause concern, as it will adjust itself when regular eating and drinking habits are resumed. One should very definitely not take any laxatives under such conditions, as such medication depletes the system of moisture already in it.

What to do if Water is Scarce

If we have ample water at the moment but may have little or none later, the soundest procedure will be to drink as much as we reasonably can before quitting the source of supply. We should fill up, for example, if we have the opportunity to do so before abandoning a ship or plane. If we are in dry country, it will be a good idea unless there are extenuating circumstances to drink a lot while at and just before leaving a water hole.

Every effort should be made to take adequate water with us when we are leaving what may be an isolated supply. This water we may want to ration and drink a little at a time, merely wetting the lips and rolling a sip around the mouth before swallowing it. Carrying something such as a button or small clean pebble in the mouth will help to decrease the sensation of thirst.

The remainder of a small supply should not be heedlessly consumed until we actually have more water, for that spectacle of sparkling lake may be a mirage, that plane may not have spied us, and a dry canyon may lie hidden between us and that river which gleams nearby.

Conserving Body Moisture

An often unbelievable amount of water is exuded through the pores of the skin, and the rate of perspiration is markedly increased both by heat and by exertion. The need of water intake can be lessened, therefore, by our keeping as quiet as possible and as comfortably cool as we can.

Keeping the clothing wet will help at sea in hot weather, although it may prove desirable to rinse the clothing during the latter part of the afternoon to prevent too much salt from accumulating and to dry out before evening if the nights are chilly.

If in arid emptiness without sufficient water and obliged to depend upon our own resources to get out, our best chance will be to stay as relaxed and cool as possible during the torrid hours. Traveling can be done during the respites of dawn and dusk and, particularly across open sands, at night.

If on flat shelterless desert, we can always scoop out a narrow pit in which to lie while the sun is blazing down. The utmost shade will be secured, as everyone appreciates, if this trench extends east and west. Two or three feet of depth can result in as much as 100° difference in temperature between its shadowy bottom and ground level. Before we take to such a refuge, we may want to leave some sign of our presence in case help passes nearby. Weighting a shirt over one of the excavated piles may serve.

When Water is Replenished

When inadequate water supplies are eventually replenished, it will be inadvisable to drink a great deal at once. If the satisfaction is extended over several hours, the body will utilize the intake to the fullest possible extent instead of sluicing it through the system and dissipating a considerable amount wastefully in rapid elimination. Even when there is suddenly all the water we can possibly want, partaking of it too rapidly and in too large amounts will cause nausea.

If We Are to Survive

Bark may be used as suggested in the preceding chapter to fashion numerous types of water-holding containers. To make a primitive basin, one handy way is to scoop a hole in soft ground and to line that with a piece of waterproof canvas, plastic, or something similar. Do we want hot water? Then we already know about scattering a few clean pebbles along the bottom of the water-filled receptacle and placing on these, perhaps with temporary tongs made by bending a green stick back up itself, stones that have been heating in the campfire.

The point is: no ordinary problem will stump any of us for very long if we possess sufficient enterprise and ingenuity to have a reasonable chance of surviving at all.

PART TWO

WARMTH

"There is usually little object in traveling tough just for the sake of being tough."

—*Hudson's Bay Company*

Chapter 10

Facts Of Lighting Fires

FEW ACTS are so immediately indicative of an individual's woodsmanship as the way he goes about lighting a fire, especially without the help of matches.

For fires can be so ignited by any of us, and if one method does not succeed there is always another, but the very fact that success is often elusive and to be achieved only laboriously is all the more reason for exerting every reasonable precaution always to have dry matches at hand.

What Matches to Carry

If we are going to make an effort to have matches readily available whenever in the wilderness, it follows that we may as well make a point of carrying the most practical matches for such purposes, and these are the long wooden variety.

Paper matches are too often an abomination in the bush. If we ever do happen to find ourselves in the Silent Places with nothing more substantial, we will want to bend every effort toward keeping them as intact from dampness as possible; and from the effects of perspiration as well as from outer wetness. Wrapping the folder in something such as foil or a handy bit of plastic will serve to protect heads and stems as well as the integral striking surface.

What About Match Cases

A waterproof match case will help to assure that a store of matches carried on the person will remain dry, particularly if this container is also unbreakable. For several years I carried one made of some hard black composition, and then one afternoon while taking Arctic grayling on a Black Gnat I slipped in midstream. What happened to that match holder was one of those inevitabilities that, as soon as they do occur, you wonder why you never considered before.

The most practical waterproof match case on the market that I have been able to find is the very well known one long put out by the Marble Arms and Manufacturing Company and retailed for less than one dollar. Any match case for woods use should have some provision by which it can be fastened safely to the person, and Marble's is built with a mobile metal ring at the top through which it can be pinned or tied. The lid is attached in such a way that it can be unscrewed easily when the hands are cold or slippery and yet can not be mislaid.

With any match holder, another danger to eschew is the accidental igniting of the matches within. That I once managed to accomplish also by too carelessly screwing on the unyielding cap of that same composition case, on the other edge of the continent this time on the Southwest Miramichi River. The sound was like that of a gun going off. It was after noticing my right hand was blackened and that the particular batch of matches was charred that I realized what had happened. The black washed off all right, not revealing even a burn, and I had more matches.

Since then, even though the top of Marble's waterproof match box has a protective rubber lining, I have been careful to stow about half with the butts up and to keep the heads of all as much apart as possible. It is thus possible to pack away more, too.

Ways to Maintain Reserves

If you spend much time back of beyond, you probably do like most of our acquaintances who are so privileged and scatter several watertight containers filled with matches throughout your duffel for possible emergency needs. You may also take the additional precaution of either sealing these holders or encasing the matches themselves with paraffin.

Because caution becomes second nature when one continues to follow wilderness trails—where a misstep that in civilization would be only temporarily annoying can, with no help at hand, totter one on the edge of disaster—you likely agree it is no more than prudent to carry an extra filled waterproof case on your person.

The Principles of Fire

There is no single way by which the campfire must be built. The principles, however, are always the same.

Firewood does not burn directly, of course. Rather it is a gas driven from the wood by heat that, in combination with the oxygen in the air, flames.

We have to start, therefore:

(1) with fuel inflammable enough,
(2) to give off gas sufficiently combustible,
(3) to be lit by the heat we are able to concentrate on it.

This burning kindling, in turn, must be amply hot and long-lived to release and inflame more and more gas from progressively larger amounts of fuel.

The heat necessary for the initial reaction is ordinarily obtained most conveniently by striking a match.

Making Fire By Striking Spark

Campfires can be lit without matches, just as game animals can be bagged without guns, cleaned without knives, and cooked without utensils. For those who have never yet had to resort to primitive measures, suppose we try the direct spark technique which is the easiest of the ancient methods.

That a suitable spark can be made by striking the back of a hunting knife against a piece of flint is well known by everyone who has read of the pioneer uses of flint and steel. Not so generally realized, except by those of more experimental natures, is that other hard stones such as quartz, jasper, iron pyrites, agate, and native jade will serve instead of the traditional flint.

Nor need a knife or even steel be used. Iron, for example, will do instead. Furthermore, if only by the process of trial and error, two rocks can generally be found that when struck together with a brisk stroking motion will give off sparks. The familiar fool's gold, iron pyrites otherwise named because of the sometimes exciting yellow flecks it contains, is a favorite in this respect among Eskimos many of whom carry two fist-size chunks with them.

If you happen to be by a down plane, sparks for starting a fire may be secured by scratching together the negative and positive wires from a live storage battery; suggesting possible methods of procedure whenever electrical power is at hand.

We must spread a preferably generous wad of tinder to catch the sparks, so that when these shower into the bed of highly inflammable matter, the area can be blown to a glow and then to flame. If the tinder is placed in the wind, natural air currents may be enough to take care of this step.

Once tinder is in flames, all we have to do is shove it under fuel already laid as for any outdoor fire.

Tinders are Numerous

Tinder is highly combustible substance in which a spark can be blown into flame, and innumerable materials of this sort have been popular in different localities since man came groping out of the cold of fireless eons. Many of these tinders were carried, and some are still borne, in special containers such as tinderboxes, pouches, horns, and other characteristic receptacles.

Birchbark can be detached in the thinnest of layers and these shredded to make tinder. The barks of some of the cedars can be similarly utilized. Dry moss, lichen, grass, and dead evergreen needles are among the additional substances pulverized for tinder. Other suitable dry materials so used are obtained from nests.

The dry fuzz from pussy willows is a well-known tinder. So is wood which has dry rotted and can be rubbed to a powder. A number of mushrooms and other fungi are dehydrated for such a purpose. The desiccated pith from the inside of elderberry shoots was employed by some Indians. So was down from milkweed, fireweed, and like vegetation.

A handful of very dry pine needles often works. You can use the fluff of the so-called cotton grass, that of the cattails, and the downy heads of such flowers as mature goldenrod. Divers dry vegetable fibers serve as tinder. So does the powdery dry droppings of bats. So does the down found in some nests and on the underneath parts of some birds.

Lighting Fires with Water and Ice

A small magnifying glass is a convenient device with which to start a fire when there is sufficient sunlight. Similar lenses, such as those used in telescopic sights and binoculars, are likewise used. A piece of ordinary glass, perhaps from a broken jar, sometimes possesses in its distortions sufficient qualities of magnification.

The magnifying properties of water can be capitalized upon for fire making by, for example:

(a) holding the crystals from two watches or pocket compasses of about the same size back to back,

(b) filling the space between with water,

(c) directing this makeshift enlarging lens so as to converge the rays of the sun in a point sharp enough to start tinder glowing.

It is possible with ingenuity to devise other such improvisations.

A satisfactory lens can also be fashioned by experimentally shaving, and then smoothing with the warm hand, a piece of clear ice.

Starting Blaze with Firearm

Pry the bullet from the cartridge, first loosening the case if you want by laying it on a log and tapping the neck all around with the back of your knife. If you are carrying a shotgun, uncrimp the top of the shell and remove the wadding and projectiles. Have the campfire laid with a good bed of tinder beneath. Pour some of the powder over this tinder.

Stuff a small bit of dry frayed cloth into what remains of the load. Fire the weapon straight up into the air. The rag, if it is not already burning when it falls nearby, should be smoldering sufficiently so that when pressed into the tinder it can be quickly blown into flame.

Obtaining Fire With Bow and Drill

Fires have long been made throughout the world from glowing embers obtained by the combined use of bow, drill, and fire board. Although the technique is simple, considerable diligence and effort are required, for its application can be very laborious. Once you've started, in other words, don't become too easily discouraged but keep going.

You'll need a bow, with a thong long enough to loop around the dry stick that is to serve as a drill. You'll need a socket with which to hold the drill against a hollow in the fire board.

By moving the bow back and forth and so rotating the drill in the fire board, you cause so much friction that a spark starts glowing in tinder amassed to catch it. This spark you blow into flame with which the campfire is lighted.

Socket

The only use of the socket is to hold the drill in place while the latter is being turned. The socket, which for this purpose is held in one hand, can be an easily grasped knot of wood with a hollow shaped in its underneath. It can be one of the smooth stones, with a slick depression worn in one side, often found near water.

The socket may be oiled or waxed to allow the drill, whose upper end should offer as little resistance as possible, to spin more freely.

What Wood to Use

Among the North American woods that are favored for making fire by friction are the poplar, tamarack, basswood,

yucca, balsam fir, red cedar, white cedar, cypress, cotton-
wood, elm, linden, and willow. The drill and the fire board
are both often made of a single one of the above woods, although this is not always the case.

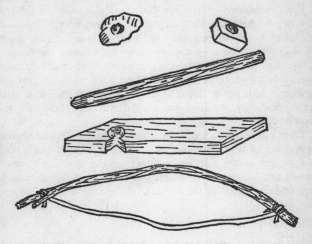

FIG. 35. Fire-making bow and drill. The parts are, top to
bottom: sockets, drill, fire board, and bow.

The Drill

The drill may well be a straight and well seasoned stick
from one-fourth to three-fourths of an inch in diameter and
some twelve to fifteen inches long. The top end should be as
smoothly rounded as possible so as to incur a minimum of
friction. The lower end, where on the other hand a maximum
of friction is desired, is more blunt.

A longer drill, perhaps one nearly a yard in length, is
sometimes rotated between the palms rather than by a bow.
The hands, maintaining as much downward pressure as possible, are rubbed back and forth over the drill so as to spin
it as strongly and as swiftly as possible. When they slip too
low, they must be shifted back to the top with as little delay

in rotatation as possible. The method, as can be appreciated once you try it, is not as effective as using a bow and socket.

Fire Board

The dimensions of the fire board, which may be split out of a dry branch, can be a matter of convenience. The board, say, may be about one inch thick and three or four inches wide. It should be long enough to be held under the foot.

Using a knife or perhaps a sharp stone, start a hole about three-fourths of an inch in from the edge of the board. Enlarge this hole, thus fitting it and the end of the drill at the same time, by turning the drill with the bow as later described.

Then cut a notch from the edge of the fire board through to the side of this cup. This slot, which is usually made wider and deeper at the bottom, will permit the hot black powder that is produced by the drilling to fall as quickly as possible into tinder massed at the bottom of the notch.

And the Bow

The bow is sometimes made from an easily handled stick such as those used to propel arrows. Other peoples, believing that the bow should have no resiliency, employ a stout section of branch with a bend already in it.

One end of the bow may have a natural crotch to facilitate the tying of the thong. The bow may merely be notched for this purpose, however, or perhaps drilled if heavy enough not to split. The bow string, which may be anything from a shoe lace to a twisted length of rawhide, is tied at both ends so as to leave enough slack to allow its being twisted once around the drill.

Using Bow and Drill

The various components when ready will roughly resemble the set shown in the drawing. They are used as illustrated, the campfire first being made ready to ignite.

The tinder is bedded under the slot in the fire board. If you're right handed, you kneel on your right knee and place the left foot as solidly as possible on the fire board.

Take the bow in the right hand, looping the string over the drill. The drill is set in the cavity prepared in the fire board.

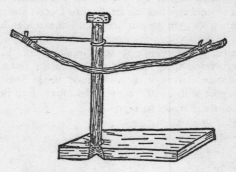

FIG. 36. Using fire bow and drill.

Pressure from the socket, which is grasped in the left hand, holds the drill in position. You can grip the socket more steadily, you will probably find, if you will keep your left wrist against your left shin and hug the left leg with that arm. Press down on the drill, but not enough to slow it, when you commence twirling the drill by sawing back and forth with the bow.

Now start drawing the bow smoothly back and forth in sweeps as long as the string will conveniently permit. Maybe you've dropped a few grains of sand into the cup to increase friction. At any rate, the hole will eventually commence to smoke. Work the bow even faster now, never stopping the swift even action. Press down more assertively on the drill.

Lighting the Fire

Hot black powder will begin to be ground out into the tinder. Keep on drilling, for the heartier a spark you can start glowing there, the quicker you'll be able to blow it into flame.

When everything seems right, gently remove the drill. Breath softly into the slot until you can actually see a gleam. Then pick up both fire board and tinder if that is easiest. Press the tinder carefully around the incandescence. When the spark definitely begins spreading, get the board out of the way so that you can fan the heat more freely. Carefully continue feeding oxygen to the area until the tinder bursts into flame.

Natives often carry fire so won, igniting for this purpose dry spongy wood that, like the punk sold for setting off fireworks, smolders over long periods of time. This fire stick they transport with them, ready to be blown into flame when the next blaze is ready to light.

Chapter 11

Speaking Of Warmth

How MUCH more interesting an event is that man's supper who has just been forth to hunt the fuel to cook it with.

The ability to build a campfire swiftly and certainly in every type of weather that may one day beset us can, at a decisive moment, also mean the difference between existence and finality; and the way to acquire such skill is a bit at a time over as long a period as possible, using on each occasion only whatever natural materials may be at hand.

From this stems the principal objection, and as I think you'll agree a grave one, against getting in the habit of un-necessarily cutting corners with any of the fire kindlers that are on the market. For there may come a blusterous winter night when the trees are bent with sleet, and the individual up against it may very well not have a chemical tablet to ignite instead of the bark and shavings to which, although they have always been available as they are now, he has not become accustomed.

Bountiful Birchbark

Snow, certainly, imposes but a scant handicap to starting a campfire in birch country. No more does rain for that matter, as you can substantiate if you have ever arbitrarily dipped birchbark into a lake, touched the pronged flame of a match to a frayed corner, and had the singular satisfaction of watching the strip still crackle into flame.

The graceful tree need not even be disfigured, for it is sheathed withl ayer after layer of tissue—thin bark, enough shreds of which can be peeled free by the fingers alone to start under favorable conditions any fire we may want to build.

Can one ever forget the first occasion when alone in the murmurous forest he heaps that initial handful on a cleared bit of ground, leans a wigwam of small dry softwood self-consciously above it, adds with increasing hesitation now a few larger sticks, and then feels deliciously stabbing his nostrils the first sweet black wisps of smoke when that single match stirringly catches hold.

When the Woods are Wet

When you are in the deep forest and it's maybe drizzling, you start with the same inflammable wisps, but next to them you lean and crisscross larger ribbons of birchbark. These can also be secured by the finger alone, although it will be easier, unless there may be a reason for not so doing, to cut the tree lengthwise, pry up a long roll of bark, and pull that around and off. The thick sheet thus obtained can be then ripped to narrow strips which will burn much more readily than would the intact section.

In more extreme circumstances, you get so that you commence almost automatically to lay a broad sheet of birchbark in as sheltered a nook as appears handy. Atop this go the shreds and the stouter fragments, and these you may cover with still larger portions. The small and then the bigger pieces of dry softwood go up in teepee formation, forming a compact but well ventilated peak through which the flames can hungrily climb. Rectangles of birchbark finally roof the pile, blocking out wind storm.

The time comes to light the match. You realize you must hold it so that whatever air currents reach it will run the flame down the match stem where will be the initial fuel on which to feed. Perhaps you'll face the wind with your two hands cupped in front of the match. Perhaps you'll elect to lie between the wind and the pile, using your body and perhaps the opened flap of a mackinaw as a barricade.

Inflammability of Evergreen Twigs

Except on those days when every branch is slick with ice, it is practically as easy to start a fire with a tight handful of small dead evergreen twigs as with birchbark. Quantities of these dead, resinous little stubs angle scratchily from the undersides of all conifers.

They may be broken off in thick uniform fistfuls, lit if desired while turned most advantageously in the hand, and finally laid down in such a way that the flames will sputter toward the center. Already gathered fuel can then be quickly angled and crisscrossed above this blazing nucleus in well aerated patterns through which fire will be able to ascend quickly.

Making and Using Fuzzsticks

Some bushmen start all fires, indoors and out, with fuzzsticks, for although in terms of initial effort they are often more bother than a handful of dry pine twigs, this shortcoming they counteract with the ingratiating characteristic of dependability. Fuzzsticks are a solution, certainly, in that most trying of weather conditions when every bit of fuel in the forest is covered with ice. You may have to go to the extra effort of splitting or breaking out firewood under such circumstances, also.

Fuzzstick is merely the colloquialism for a piece of wood to which a contrived cluster of attached shavings cling. One is easily enough made by shaving a straight-grained stick of dry, preferably split softwood with single knife strokes until one end is a mass of wooden curls.

The usual procedure is to bunch no less than three such fuzzsticks so that the flames will be able to eat into the shavings, toss on any stray whittlings, light the mass, and then go through the usual procedure of adding progressively larger firewood, allowing always for draft.

Differences in Firewood

The difference between the so-called hardwoods and soft-woods is, as you already understand, a matter of botany, having nothing to do with grain, texture, or weight; for is not yew which is a softwood tougher than many a hardwood oak? Softwoods come from coniferous trees such as pines, tamaracks, firs, spruces, and cedars. Hardwoods are derived from the trees that, instead of needles or scales, have the various familiar types of flat leaves.

The resinous softwoods when seasoned generally make the best kindling. They catch and burn quickly. They are smoky, however, short lived, and prone to throw sparks. They are most valuable, in other words, when either we wish to start a fire or when we desire a fast brief blaze.

The seasoned hardwoods in most cases provide both a steadier and a longer lasting fire. They are particularly suitable for most cooking, as they disintegrate into hot enduring coals that afford the intense even heat usually then desirable. When we can, therefore we'll probably start most of our fires with softwood and hold them with hardwood.

What Wood to Use

We do not have to build many campfires before learning that when dry fuel is called for, fallen wood that has absorbed moisture from the ground should be avoided. About the only time this is worth bothering with, unless fuel is scarce, is when it is desirable to keep a fire going for a long period without very much heat.

Standing deadwood is what we ordinarily come to seek, and we soon realize there are varying degrees of quality even in this. An upright stump that is rotten is of little value except to hold a fire, although we can occasionally uncover a tough resinous core in decayed softwood that will burn as if long soaked in oil. Dead birch, on the other hand, quickly loses most heat producing ability if the bark remains intact to hold in the moisture.

A few green woods, such as birch and white ash, burn best when alive. By splitting out kindling and making fuzzsticks, you find you can even start a fire with either one. Green wood in general, however, is best used mixed with dry.

Some of the barks, such as that of hemlock, are valuable for giving off steady warmth. Experimentation with what happens to be at hand seems usually to be the best teacher, for the same species of wood vary to some extent in different parts of the continent because of soil and atmospheric conditions. Among each family group, too, are often many separate types each with its peculiar characteristics.

Hickory leads the North American firewoods in heat producing ability. Oak is not far behind. Beech ranks next in numerous areas, closely followed by the birches and maples. Ash is a favorite with many of us. So is elm. Then come tamarack, yellow pine, chestnut, poplar, white pine, and spruce.

Much depends on where we happen to be at the moment. In some eastern localities we've burned mostly birch, while the woodpiles that take us comfortably through sixty-below-zero stretches in the Canadian Rockies are mainly poplar and lodgepole pine. Some sections have to get along with the poorer oaks, such as willow oak, which are among the least effective hardwoods in caloric energy.

You'll naturally do the best you can, remembering the general rule that the heavier a wood is, the greater is its heating potential.

Ways of Conserving Energy

Although there are any number of often ingenious ways to make little sticks out of big limbs without the use of either knife or ax, the point remains that frequently it is easier, and therefore at least under emergency conditions preferable, to burn firewood in two instead of expending energy unnecessarily in otherwise sectioning it. One other strength-conserving dodge is to lay the ends of long sticks in the blaze, continuing to advance them as they are consumed.

Another pertinent factor often overlooked in this connection is the fact that a long fire is very often preferable. If you want an open fire to lie beside, for example, it should be at least as long as your body.

Suppose we wish to cook with several utensils at the same time? Perhaps we'll want to suspend these above a long slim conflagration, from a green pole laid between two crotched sticks.

Possibly we will prefer to set them, instead, in some steady position where they'll get sufficient heat. Two of the simplest ways to go about achieving this will be to build a long narrow fire, either in a narrow trench or between two green logs laid closely enough together so that the pots can straddle them.

To take advantage of the best available draft, a long fire should be laid in a line with prevalent air currents. When the fire is confined by two logs, these may be advantageously placed in a slim V with the open end toward the wind.

Sleeping Warm While Siwashing

We can build a long large fire, brush it carefully to one side when ready to retire, and then strech out on the warmed ground.

We may also want to consider the merit of heating stones in the fire for use as substitute hot water bottles, being wary of any which have been in or near water. Attractively smooth rocks from stream beds are particular offenders, the fluid often trapped within them expanding to steam and thus causing sometimes dangerous explosions.

If the weather is at all cold, we will owe it to ourselves to take the fullest possible advantage of reflected heat, and although it does not take anyone long to appreciate the efficacy of kindling a night fire against some radiating surface such as a flat boulder, to comprehend the value of having such a reflector behind us is usually a matter of far greater experience.

One of the ways in the Far North to distinguish a cheechako from a sourdough is to watch how the stranger arranges his heating fire. The newcomer kindles his blaze, however expertly, against a cliff and sits in front of it. The oldtime Northerner builds his fire farther away from the rock face and sits between the cliff and the fire.

Night Fire

The nuisance of being unexpectedly caught out in the bush overnight is that if we need a fire, we'll probably have to rouse up a dozen times or so to add fresh fuel. The redeeming feature is that the chore is not as disagreeable in fact as it may be in theory.

You sleep until deepening cold slowly awakens you, and then, likely as not, you roll closer to the companionship of the embers. Although you can thus win an extra few minutes of repose, eventually you have to stir sufficiently to draw sticks from the pile you've heaped within arms' reach. Flames lick around them, sketching a thousand flamboyant pictures while returning heat brings with it relaxing lassitude.

If you happen to have an ax (you can make a fairly efficient job of preparing a night fire. One satisfactory method is to pound a couple of green poles into the ground behind the fire from which they slant. You pile a single wall of green logs against these. The theory is that as the lowest log disintegrates, the one above will replace it.

The operation seldom works out this automatically, but you should still enjoy a considerable quantity of reflected heat which will need feeding only a few times during the night, and which at dawn will still boast enough coals so that over them you can cook breakfast—or at least toast your hands while coming awake.

Building Campfire in Extreme Cold

During extremely cold spells, one will ordinarily be advised to find the best shelter available and to lay up beside a fire until the frost moderates.

When vitality starts ebbing and a chill begins to spread

throughout the body, one needs nourishment or rest, and preferably both. It is poor policy to keep traveling on nerve unless the distance to be traversed is short and the possible gain to be derived by covering it proportionately large. The best axiom, sourdoughs find, is to get a fire going and eat. If food is lacking, the next best thing to do is to keep as warm and as inactive as possible until the cold breaks.

Everything should be ready for the fire before the hands are uncovered. The fingers will probably, be nearly stiff, anyway. If flames do not commence licking upward almost immediately once hands are bared, they should be shoved against the skin to warm before another attempt is essayed. As soon as the fingers are limber enough to hold a match, the try can be made again as swiftly and certainly as possible.

Other Fuels

If where we are no trees are growing, driftwood may be your best fuel. If above the timber line, we may still be able to find enough stunted bushes to serve our purposes. On the plains we come to utilize small brush, roots of vegetation such as the mesquite, knots of grass, and the dry cattle refuse which is the modern equivalent of the pioneer's buffalo chips.

In some country we just naturally fall into the habit of pocketing tinder for the next fire when we come across it, while in a few regions we gather fuel itself whenever it is happened upon.

In parts of the Arctic where there does not happen to be driftwood, coal and peat are occasionally to be secured. Roots and brush are frequently available. The small heather-like evergreen known as cassiope is sufficiently resinous to burn while wet and green. Moss and lichen can also be used as fuels. All may be secured from beneath the snow if necessary.

To Burn or to Eat

Animal hair and hides will provide warmth. So will bones and fat, the latter in some instances being laid in strips over a small pile of the former and the starting flame and heat furnished perhaps by a mass of moss until oil begins to run over the bones and to burn.

Another way to burn animal fat or oil is to place it in a container, suspend or hang in it a wick of some dry vegetation or perhaps of fishline braided for the purpose, and once the latter has soaked up enough fluid to light it.

A stove for burning oil can be made from a metal container such as a kerosene tin by:

(1) punching a hole in one side above the fuel level to serve as an air vent,

(2) making a wick with a rag or by experimenting with plant and other available substances,

(3) suspending this wick inside the container by means of a snare wire or a strip of metal cut from the can itself.

(4) and finally lighting the wick once it has become saturated with oil, first melted if need be by outside heat.

None of these animal substances should be burnt, certainly, when any may be needed more for clothing or for food. This, as we have seen, holds particularly true in the case of fat.

Chapter 12

Shelter For The Making

WHERE WE are, with what we have, right now! A fallen tree is often at hand, even when we are looking for one, under whose roots a browse bed can be laid so as to benefit from the luxury of a crackling night blaze, nor is it unusual to come upon a dry indentation in a stream bank that can be quickly roofed with brush and cheered by a campfire in front.

No canopy is more pleasant under favorable conditions than the open sky. The only refinements we want on such nights, if indeed we desire any, are a mattress of evergreen boughs, a long hardwood fire, and maybe behind us a log to reflect warmth onto those portions not turned toward the friendly heat.

On other occasions—when there is storm, or cold, or when the situation is such that our every reasonable long range effort should be directed at conserving the utmost vigor—the time and energy required for throwing up a bivouac may well be returned several fold.

Under circumstances when it may be desirable or perhaps obligatory to remain in one area, we may as well enjoy the sanctuary that for a combination of reasons is the best reasonably available. This will be especially true if sufficient food is at least temporarily lacking, for then we may expect strength to be maintained in direct proportion to our ability to remain comfortably and warmly relaxed.

Capitalizing on Caves

Not long ago I had the good fortune to spend part of a summer in company with an anthropologist from one of the great museums, trying to find in the northwestern mountains some irrefutable evidence of man's first arrival on this continent. There are, as we all realize, only clues and not proof that he may have originally crossed from Asia to the Americas in search of food. It may have been the other way around.

One theory is that during a glacial era some two hundred centuries ago, ocean levels were lowered perhaps a hundred yards to reveal a dry land bridge in the vicinity of Bering Strait. Any Asians traversing such a course to Alaska may well have hunted southward for meat.

If there are any actual traces of such a trek, these are hidden amid the valleys and ranges wrought by four Ice Ages, for unrelieved cold such as that which now makes the Antarctic a dead continent apparently soon again gripped the Arctic. It was probably about the time of Christ that the first relations of the modern Eskimo came groping toward his present home, out of the twilight of the most recent frozen era.

What we sought that trip were shallow caves where earlier Americans could have tarried in comparative ease with a fire kindled comfortably in front. The most likely type of caves we did locate were on my own land, as a matter of fact, a few feet above the Peace River which aborigines might well have followed after traveling south down the Continental Trough.

Temporary shelters today are distinguished by the same qualities that would have made them desirable during the Stone Age. We want somewhere dry, protected from wind, safe, and preferably small enough to be easily heated. Such natural bivouacs are happened upon everywhere in the wild and rural areas of North America.

Dangers From Carbon Monoxide

Carbon monoxide is a potential threat in any closed space, be this cabin or hut or tent, where there is a fire of any kind. Even a blaze in a tight new stove with adequate drafts may be dangerous, for the heat-reddened metal itself can release dangerous amounts of the poisonous gas.

Carbon monoxide—which is a product of incomplete combustion, being the ever present carbon dioxide except for one missing atom of oxygen per molecule—is a particularly insidious gas because of its characteristics of being odorless and cumulative. The ill effects of breathing small amounts of the usually unsuspected poison day after day accumulate slowly in the body until one more perhaps otherwise inconsequential dose lays the victim low.

It seldom gives any recognizable warning. There is no difficulty with breathing, for instance. What generally occurs is that one is so suddenly overcome that when first he does realize something is wrong, he is already nearly if not entirely helpless.

Carbon monoxide has killed many in the wilderness. The best preventative is to make sure of good ventilation. There is even very real danger in a tent, for if the spaces in the weave of the fabric are closed either by waterproofing or by frost, to give two common examples, a small heater can and in many recorded cases has killed all occupants.

Danger is increased as cold deepens because of the human tendency to restrict ventilation in favor of warmth. Poor circulation of air not only permits the invisible and odor-free gas to accumulate in a closed area, but the very fact that the atmosphere becomes progressively more and more stale itself tends to increase the formation of carbon monoxide by not affording sufficient oxygen for complete combustion.

The Death Awaiting Parked Motorists

While on the subject of carbon monoxide, it may save lives to draw attention here to the particular peril that awaits motorists stalled by snow and ice. The tendency under such conditions is to keep windows tightly shut and the motor going so as to heat the car. The danger when any closed vehicle is so parked, particularly if a white smother of flakes is building up around the conveyance, is that carbon monoxide can and many times does collect inside the unventilated automobile in killing quantities.

Emergency Treatment

What is the emergency treatment in remote areas for carbon monoxide poisoning? Get outdoors with the very least possible delay, or at least get in a position where you can breathe fresh air even if this means slashing or smashing something. Keep warm.

As soon as you are able to do so without too much risk of being overcome, eliminate the cause. If for example this is a wood stove whose drafts have been too tightly closed, open the outlets as wide as possible and, of course, get fresh air into the shelter and from then on keep it particularly well ventilated.

Drink some stimulant such as hot tea, coffee, or chocolate if you have it. Take it as easy as you can for awhile, lying quietly in blankets or eider down if possible, breathing deeply to help rid the blood of the effects of the poison.

Coniferous Shelters

No one needs have much difficulty in finding sanctuary in softwood country, for no ax is necessary and, in fact, we can get along very well without even a knife.

A heavy grove of big evergreens itself affords considerable shelter. How many times during a sudden shower have we kept dry by lingering under a spruce or pine, and on how many occasions in snow belts have we avoided deep going by keeping as much as possible to tall thick stands of conifers? There is usually sufficient small growth in such forests to break off and angle in lean-to form against a protective log or trunk.

On those occasions when we may find ourselves among low spruce and fir, few things are simpler than to make a niche by stripping off a few lower branches from a well situated tree. These boughs, augmented by others from nearby trees, will quickly floor and thatch the shelter. Such a nook is particularly easy to heat with the plethora of fuel almost always available in such terrain.

If a blizzard is scuffing or rain dripping and some easily handled bark such as that from birch trees is available, we'll probably want to insert a few sheets at least overhead. For bedding, a soft mass of additional boughs sandwiched between such waterproofing bark can furnish surprising comfort even when the world is restless with wet and cold.

What if There's Snow?

Snow can make the task of bivouacking even easier. Suppose we're traveling along a wilderness river. There may be boulders along the shore between which snow walls can be heaped and over them several young evergreens spread. Among the driftwood likely at hand, there's apt to be some large dry snags which, when a conflagration is kindled against them, will themselves burn with the help of enough occasional extra fuel to keep them going.

Another way to get by is to tunnel into sufficiently deep snow, taking care to do this at right angles to the wind so that there will be less chance of the opening's being choked by drift.

Still another procedure when snow lies heavy is to open a crude hole from the top down. Such a trench can often be made by stamping. It may be in the shape of a rough triangle with the wider end, roofed and floored with evergreen, large enough to sit or curl up in and with the narrower part reflecting a small fire.

Precautions With Snow

We'll naturally want to avoid making a snow camp where there may be danger from rapidly forming drifts, from overhang, or from slides.

If in open country, we will beware of making the shelter

on the side of an elevation that is protected from the wind. Taking such a precaution is exactly opposite from what we would do in the forest, but in open terrain such lees gather drifts that can bury and suffocate one.

Keeping dry is particularly important under such conditions, inasmuch as clothing that becomes damp or frozen quickly loses its qualities of insulation. Instead of our sitting or lying in direct contact with snow, it will be safer to have some protective material between, and this may be an oilskin gamebag, section of plastic, mitts, or any handy bark.

Houses of Snow

An easy way to go about constructing a snow house in very cold weather, as you may have already proved to yourself, is to heap snow in a mound slightly larger than the enclosure desired. Pack down the final surface. If the weather is well below freezing and if water is at hand, throw that over the pile so that a glaze of ice will be formed. Otherwise, let the mound harden as well as it will in the air for a half-hour or so.

Fig. 37. Snow Burrow.

Then burrow into the pile at right angles to the wind. Keep scooping out snow until as thin a shell as seems feasible remains. Build a small blaze within| Any melt will be blotted up by the snow remaining. Drag out embers and ashes finally, poke a ventilation hole through the dome, and allow the shelter to ice.

A very small fire within such a snow house, augmented by body heat, will keep the temperature surprisingly comfortable. The tendency, in fact, will probably be toward overheating. Extremely important in any event will be the maintenance of good ventilation.

Shelter for the Making

"A comfortable house was once made here," said Thoreau, "almost entirely of such materials as Nature furnished."

Chapter 13

Wilderness Homes

WE FREQUENTLY HAVE the opportunity of camping where the temperature is either warmer or cooler than that of the surrounding country. The reasons permitting this freedom of choice are well known to everyone who considers the result of air's becoming heavier as it loses heat, and who, perhaps, can even visualize it flowing as it does like water into low hollows and through ravines and canyons.

If we are traveling in mountainous country without bedding when nights are chilly, we're apt to be able to sleep more comfortably in a sheltered spot partway down the lee slope of a hill than in a valley. On the other hand, the currents of cool air that follow streams are particularly agreeable in warmer weather when instead we are seeking relief from heat. Such breezes, too, are valuable in blowing away annoying insects.

Where Not to Camp

Selecting a suitable camp site is not too complicated a problem when the main objective is less one of pleasure than of survival. Common sense is the principal determinant, for it is no more than reasonable to expect drinking water and firewood ordinarily to be at hand. If we are stranded or in some other difficulty where we will appreciate any help that may be along, we'll naturally pick a spot that is as conspicuous as possible.

We will not decide upon a site in any event that may be inundated by a suddenly rising stream, particularly not if we are aware of the disastrous results in some areas of storms not even visible locally. Warning tokens to be considered often include scars and debris left by previous high water.

Lush growth may be not only rough and soggy underfoot, but it may presage troublesome insects. We'll try to avoid places where there may be cave-ins, avalanches, or peril from tumbling rocks. If there is any danger of electrical storms, we will also remember that solitary trees have a tendency to attract lightning.

Particularly to be shunned will be jeopardy from falling timber. Such trees as cottonwoods and poplars are particular offenders when it comes to unexpectedly tumbling limbs. The fast growing coastal pines of California are extremely brittle and, therefore, threats in every sort of weather. Whenever there is any question, we'll bivouac among small growth or in the open. That is where we will make any winter camps in treeless northern regions, well away from lees where drifting snow can be an insidious hazard.

Anyone Can Build a Lean-To

The lean-to built as an emergency shelter will be essentially a simple frame on which is hung, leaned, lashed, pinned, woven, or otherwise affixed such covering as may be available.

A lot of us, for example, may have gone about putting up a temporary shelter of this sort by driving two forked sticks into the ground about seven feet apart and laying a pole between the two crotches. Our second step would then have consisted of making a pup tent-like enclosure by angling large evergreen boughs from ridgepole to ground along each side. Finally, we would have closed at least one end, perhaps by laying several small firs against it.

More complicated frames are easily enough assembled, particularly when the joints are fastened if only by lashing them with fine but tough spruce roots, or with wiry birch or willow withes. Natural forks can be used instead, however. So can braces. Although a knife will simplify the task, not even that is necessary.

The skeleton can then be draped, interlaced, or otherwise covered with green branches, bark, moss, grass, reeds, leafy vines, and other such materials.

The few basic principles are self evident. When thatching a roof, as we may do with bark, we will naturally start at the eaves and lay the bottom of each succeeding layer across the top of the thickness beneath, so that any water will tend to flow unimpeded off the edge. If we happen to build a roof with a double pitch, we'll further waterproof that by bending bark over the ridge and fastening or weighting it down on each slant.

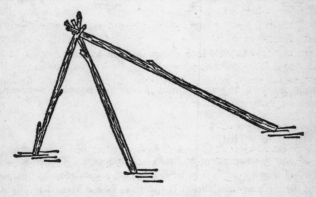

FIG. 38. Lean-to frame.

When thatching the walls, we will of course commence at the bottom as if shingling and work up, layer by layer, with each higher series always covering the top of the one immediately below. Water will then be more apt to run down the outside of the structure instead of into it.

Going About the Construction

Probably the most satisfactory way to describe a few of the more common types of lean-tos is by means of the following self-explanatory illustration. From them, even the newest frequenter of the woods can figure out the most practical way to use whatever wilderness materials happen to be at hand.

If we've something such as a tarpaulin to stretch over a pole framework, our work will be considerably lessened. This will also be true to a considerable extent if only the roof can thus be quickly rendered waterproof. A large rectangle of plastic, folded and carried in a shirt pocket, is not a bad

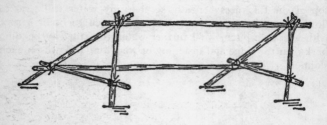

FIG. 39. More elaborate lean-to frame.

thing to take along at all times if only for possible emergency use as a rainy day cover.

Why Not a Hut?

It may be expedient to build an emergency shelter so substantial that its walls can be additionally insulated by heaping sod or earth against them. If these walls are leaned in slightly from the bottom, gravity will tend to hold such reinforcements more firmly.

The roof can also be rendered warmer by covering it with several inches of vegetation, topped by enough dirt or preferably more durable sod to keep everything in place. An animal skin, some contrivance of woven vines, or perhaps an available fabric may be hung over an opening to serve as a door.

An open stone fireplace can be made in the center of the

dirt floor of such a shelter. Although a chimney hole will then have to be cut in the roof for ventilation, this vent may be kept covered when the fire is entirely out. It should not be closed otherwise because of the threat of carbon monoxide poisoning.

Door in Relation to Wind

When the wind is any problem, the opening of a temporary shelter is usually placed on the side away from it. In open snow country where blocking drifts may form in that lee, however, the entrance is best built crosswise to the wind. This

Fig. 40. Thatching lean-to.

is also the most satisfactory compromise when one is camped where air currents alternate up and down, as in canyons and along mountain streams.

If we are putting up a structure that may be used for several days or longer, we will not be governed too much in this matter by the direction in which any breezes may be blowing at the moment. We will be more apt to look around for natural signs, such as deadfall and leaning trees, which will indicate the quarter of the prevailing wind.

To Ditch or Not

We may want to ditch the survival shelter so as to conduct away water that, depending on the terrain, might otherwise soak the floor. Any such drain should be placed so that in addition to other functions it will catch any moisture running down the walls.

A channel several inches wide and as deep may be made with a sharp stick in lieu of a handier tool. If this furrow is in the way of foot traffic as it may be at the front, or if the ground is such that it will crumble easily, the drain's usefulness may be maintained by filling it loosely with small stones.

If our shelter is on a slope, water will of course have to be shunted only from the upper sides. If we are camped on sand or in forest so carpeted with vegetation that water sinks into it almost immediately, no ditching at all may be necessary.

Browse Bed

There are many wilderness materials on which it is pleasant to sleep. If we want, we can make a rectangular enclosure by securing with stakes four poles in the shape we wish the bed to be. This form we can fill with aromatic pine needles, dry moss, leaves, ferns, or sweet marsh hay. The result, however, will not be the famous browse bed about which most of us have heard.

We can simplify the matter and toss a few armfuls of evergreen boughs beneath a pine tree, after having first prepared the ground by kicking flat any hummocks and by scooping out hip and shoulder holes. The result will still not be the renowned browse bed.

The construction of that requires a great deal more systematic effort. We'll need, first of all, a probably surprising quantity of the softest available boughs. Among the best for the purpose are the small young branches of the heavily needled balsam, but fir and even spruce will do nearly as well. These boughs can in the absence of knife and ax be stripped off by hand. They can be easily carried if laid one by one over a long stick which has an upward angling fork at its bottom, whereupon interlocking needles will hold the light although bulky load in place.

The operation is commenced by placing a thick layer of resilient green boughs at the head of the bed. These we lay with their underneaths upward. They are placed, in other words, opposite from the way they grow. The butts are kept well covered and pointing toward the bottom of the bed. The browse bed is thatched in this manner with row after row of boughs until it is a foot or more thick, whereupon it is reinforced and leveled by the poking in of soft young evergreen tips wherever an opening can be found.

"The first night on such a bed is a sleep-lulling, aromatic ecstasy that everyone should experience at least once," as Vena and I suggested in *How to Build Your Home in the Woods*. "The second night will be a bit bumpy. After the third night, one will feel inclined to attempt renovations with an ax load of fresh boughs."

Dome Structures

Even if no wood large enough for the ordinary lean-to is available, we can still make a very comfortable structure from growth as slight as willow.

Let us obtain first a quantity of the longest wands we can find. We can then, after examining them, draw a rough outline of the house. This, at most, should not ordinarily be much wider than the average length of the material.

The base of such a structure may be oval. It may be rectangular, in which case the final shelter may well resemble a barrel split lengthwise. Whatever the general conformation, in other words, we will find it advantageous structurally to employ rounded sides and roof.

Let us commence by securing the larger end of one wand

in the ground on the outline there scratched, which for purposes of illustration let us assume is a circle. Opposite the first wand on the round line, let us set the bigger end of the second switch. We can then draw the two tops together in the middle and tie them with roots, string, vines, rawhide, or any convenient material.

FIG. 41. Dome structure.

Let us similarly set and bend another two wands so that above the center of the circle they cross the first arch at right angles. At this apex we will lash all four together. The curve of the dome roof, now defined, will govern the decreasing size of subsequent arches.

A few inches away, or perhaps as much as a foot or so if our covering is to be canvas or light skins, we may make a slightly lower arch parallel to the first. This we may cross at right angles with a similar arch. This crisscrossing operation we may continue in such a fashion except to allow for an entrance, tying each of the numerous joints, until the frame is sufficiently sturdy.

There need be no particular methodicalness, however, for functional variations are as numerous as materials and situations. If additional supports are later needed, these can be added as necessary.

We may weave moss or grass through the final basketlike framework in lieu of anything better, perhaps laying on a second coat which can be both secured and insulated with a thick plastering of mud and snow.

Serenity

"Most men are needlessly poor all their lives because they think they must have a house as their neighbors have. Consider," suggested Thoreau, "how slight a shelter is absolutely necessary."

Chapter 14

Choice Of Clothing

THE NECESSARIES OF LIFE are food, shelter, warmth, and clothing. When we have obtained these, it is claimed, there is an alternative to struggling for the luxuries. That's to adventure on life itself, our vacation from humbler toil having commenced.

With such philosophy not everyone will agree, although I was fortunate enough to find no reason for disputing it when I went to the wilderness to live, and it may at least answer the questions of a few to note that we have never regretted the decision not to waste what are called the best years of life earning money in order to enjoy a questionable freedom during the least valuable part.

The sequence of events precipitated by this determination included the resignation from an editorial position, departure from a city which in my case happened to be Boston, and the heading with duffel bags to where meat would be free for the hunting, fish for the catching, fuel for the felling, land for the settling, and a home for the fun of building.

The wilderness will even furnish clothing, we found, although the gift is in the same category as that involving the ability to build fires without matches. Whenever possible in some matters, it is expeditious to accept as much of an assist from civilization as may be available, without becoming help-lessly dependent on anything that at some time may not be obtainable.

Wool or What?

The chances are that most of us will have had a certain latitude of choice as to the clothing we may be wearing if ever thrown upon our own resources to live as best we can off the country. We will certainly have a freedom of selection in the matter of garb to be included in any survival kit we may decide to have ready for grabbing up, if need be, at a moment's notice.

Tastes and circumstances vary. So, assuredly, do means. There are certain general considerations, however, that may profitably be taken into account.

Virgin wool, to evaluate materials broadly, is generally the safest choice for at least outer clothing if keeping warm is likely to be any problem. Even during such an extreme pro-cedure as tracking a canoe up through rapids too shallow for poling, wool clings warmly as contrasted to the clamminess of synthetics and cottons. How heavy the woolen fabric should be will depend to a large extent on climate.

A Mistake to Avoid

It is not reasonable to say to buy this or to take that, for body thermostats vary, this being one reason why some of us can not seem to become adjusted to the tropics, while others are in proportion just as miserable in polar regions.

An error to avoid in any event is the very common mistake of dressing too warmly in cold weather. The body, as we all know, regulates its temperature to a large extent with perspi-ration. Not only is the rate of such perspiring increased by clothing that is too warm, but unless the garb is loose and open enough to permit the escape of this moisture, it can in cold climes freeze within the garments. The result at best will be uncomfortable, while at worst it can so nullify qualities of insulation as to be fatal.

It follows, therefore, that in frigid weather one's clothes should be shaken and brushed as free as possible of both external and internal frost, as well as of any other moisture congealed or otherwise, before one approaches heat. When an individual can do so, clothing should furthermore under such conditions be removed and dried each night.

Waterproofs

Waterproof raiment, as for example an oil-silk shirt so thin that it may be easily carried in a breast pocket, can if you are at all active make you a lot more uncomfortably wet in a very short time than you'd get by staying out in the rain for a much longer period in an ordinary mackinaw.

Except in cold weather when such a result can be fatal or under circumstances when by undermining strength it can be dangerous, the matter has to do with individual ideas of comparative disagreeableness and is one of personal choice.

Footwear

It is not to be presumed that we do not all have our own rightful preferences, but the subject of footwear is such a fundamental one that perhaps a few specific observations may be helpful for personal evaluation in the light of your own experiences.

The feet assume an unusual importance when one is in remoter regions, and this becomes even more apparent if they are the only means of transportation on which one can depend to reach safety. Feet, too, are especially vulnerable. They are more sensitive to cold, for example, than other parts of the body:

(1) because of poorer circulation,

(2) and because the frigidity which reaches them by conduction is not only directly chilling, but is also indirectly so as a result of the condensation it causes.

Under ordinary conditions you, too, will probably prefer

either rubber or composition soles, particularly if you've had much experience with the way leather slips all over the place in the bush.

As for footwear itself where a great deal of walking is involved, sneakers can neither be depended upon to afford sufficient protection in rough going, nor to hold up under emergency conditions. At the other extreme, leather knee boots have never worked out for most of us, being heavier and clumsier than we have found functional. Seven inches from bottom of heel to top of back is normally just about the maximum functional height for footwear to be worn while covering long distances across wild terrain.

Particularly unsatisfactory for much walking are the shorter rubber boots sold for hunting, and not only because of their tendency to be either too hot or too cold. It has always seemed less uncomfortable, to me at least, to risk getting the feet wet from the outside rather than scaldingly and inevitably from within.

Although there is admittedly no one ideal foot covering to go over the always desirable best quality wool sox, that which I have most worn in widely separated parts of the continent throughout all seasons are lightweight rubberbottom boots with leather tops. The height of these tops has run as high as ten inches in wet country, but also as low as six inches whenever the terrain has made this practical. Such boots keep the feet reasonably dry. By varying the spacing and the tightness of the lacing you can maintain different degrees of ventilation. The uppers protect ankles from brush and snags and, even when loosely tied with the tops of light woolen stockings folded down over them, they keep out debris that would soon cause blisters. Such boots seldom require much if any breaking in, although with some models the unaccustomed pressure on the large Achilles' tendon at the heel may be a temporary problem which can be met, incidentally, by inserting a stiffener such as birchbark, moss, or folded paper.

Perhaps as many of us do you'll want innersoles, leather ones with steel arch supports that can be adjusted by the fingers. Two pairs of sox may be desirable for their warmth and for their cushioning effect. When we're ready to hit the trail, boots should fit so comfortably that feet and toes can move freely.

Good light leather boots with six or seven inch tops and rubber or composition soles are widely popular, too, being preferable to rubberbottom leathers when wetness is no problem and when rocky going and temperatures very much below zero are.

A Crippling Error

Sizes proper for the comparatively sedentary and smoothly paved city life will cripple you in the foot-swelling exertion of wilderness walking. Hiking footwear should be one full size longer and wider than ordinary shoes when combined with thin or medium-weight wool stockings.

Heavy wool stockings will add an additional half size to each of these aforesaid measurements; a full size if fractional gradations are not obtainable. With the often extra socks of cold weather travel, the same ratio of looseness should be maintained, and this you can best determine by trial fittings.

Leather footwear should then be broken in, preferably well in advance of regular use. The quickest satisfactory way of going about this is to stand in four inches of water for a quarter of an hour, and then to hike until the leather dries on your feet.

Stockings

Wool is what most of us want when it comes to stockings. Other materials, including nylon and similar durable synthetics, have a tendency to slip uncomfortably on the feet, while at best they will not absorb perspiration. If wool does not happen to agree with an individual, however, light socks of one of these latter materials will do for wearing next to the skin.

Only a good quality wool is worth taking into the bush, for loosely twisted yarns and slackly knit weaves soon wear out, while cheaply processed wool is also apt to be rough with burrs and other impurities that can cause sore feet. Cheap woolens tend, also, to shrink and mat excessively when washed, and this is a particularly grievous fault inasmuch as putting on clean stockings at least once each day is such easy and effective insurance against foot troubles.

If you don't have a spare pair along and the weather isn't too cold, you can still have clean stockings daily. If your feet are becoming wet anyway, you may as well wash the stockings as best you can once or twice during the day, then squeeze (not wring) them as dry as possible and put them back on. Or you can wait until ready to turn in before such laundering and, if you have no better way, draw them back on until dry.

So many dyes run during the harsh treatment to which stockings are commonly and necessarily subjected that it is safest to pick a white or natural grey.

A Handy Dodge

Wyndham Smith, husky bushman who when Vena and I met him was carrying the back of a piece of mining machinery while four ordinary men were toting the front, told us over a bear mulligan that evening that his solution to the stocking problem was to purchase apparel of this sort by the yard.

What he bought, Scotty explained, was woolen tubing similar to elongated stocking legs. All he then had to do was tie pieces of string around the bottoms of two such tubes and draw them on like ordinary stockings.

When what amounted to the heel of one tube wore through, Scotty remarked that he twisted it around so that the hole was over his instep. He had found with true Edinburgh canniness that by using the initial hole as a guide and subsequently turning it first to one side and later to the other, he could wear each tube in four different positions without mending. Nor, imparted Wyndham Smith, was that all. He finally cut off the entire section that had served as the foot, retied the string, and began the process anew.

Because the same principle can also be employed with

ordinary stockings, it is not a bad dodge to remember in an emergency.

Trousers and Such

The most satisfactory course to follow with all clothing to be worn in the wilderness is to obtain, whenever possible, raiment that has been especially and conscientiously made for hard use under primitive conditions. The harder weaves pick up less debris and withstand severe usage longer and more satisfactorily.

A primary rule with trousers and similar vesture is if we are going to be afoot to avoid tightness, particularly at the knees. This weighs the evidence against riding breeches and jodhpurs, although particularly for women, who as a sex do not have as large a selection of outdoor garb to choose from, ski wear affords many satisfactory choices both as to style and function.

Breeches made especially for the woods fit more functionally inside boots than do some other garments. They are thus out of the way where they can not hook on a snag and throw one. The legs do not become draggled in wet going, and furthermore they afford much more complete protection against insects.

If the ordinary type of trousers is worn, the majority of us will soon agree that cuffs serve no useful purpose in the bush. Neither do long trouser legs, and furthermore they can cause bad falls by catching in undergrowth. A common procedure in the forest is to slash off these tubes about halfway to the knee. This is what is known as stagging.

A great many individuals especially in horse country prefer levis and similar dungarees, with long underwear beneath varying according to the weather, and such hard weaves stand up best in mountainous rocky going.

The fabric chosen may well be water resistant, not waterproof, if only to keep it from becoming too heavy with wetness. Whether hunting or not, most of us like a soft enough material to permit quiet progress without a lot of noisy scratching and scraping.

The Belt to Buy

It is reasonable to desire every article selected for possible use under survival conditions to be functional in as many ways as feasible. An example is the belt which, although suspenders are admittedly more comfortable for supporting the heavier loads one pockets in the woods, most of us choose to retain trousers and breeches.

A light dressy band will serve the primary purpose, but a more rugged article with a stoutly attached buckle may one day be invaluable for lowering one safely from a precarious foothold, for suspending a deer out of the way of bears by strapping its neck to a temporarily bent sapling, and for the numerous other odd tasks that arise when one is in the wilderness.

One, Two, and Three Shirts

Preferably they should be shirts made for the job and with pockets, both capacious and capable of being securely fastened, which will make it easier to carry safely the numerous small items one is always needing in the farther places.

You may prefer a shirt that fits snugly, although one that is loose affords more protection from insects. A convenient place to stow a small bundle, too, is between such an ample shirt and the back; unless the shirt has a game pocket which, of course, is more convenient still.

A rugged cotton shirt is what you'll perhaps want in certain regions and during particular seasons. A resilient virgin wool garment, closely woven of tightly and uniformly spun fine yarns, with two large high pockets that have buttoned flaps is excellent for cooler going.

In cold weather, you can wear two of these shirts. For windproofing, a loosely fitting top garment of finespun unbleached cotton will afford sufficient ventilation to deter the collecting and condensing of body moisture.

Because of the insulation afforded by confined air, two or three layers of light clothing are more comfortable and effective than a single garment containing the same weight of materials. There is also the added advantage of adaptability. You can always unbutton or remove shirts one by one, as you may desire to do during a warm afternoon or when you begin perspiring too rapidly soon after the start of a sub-zero trek.

Shirts on Desert

A light woolen shirt will not be out of place under most desert conditions, being valuable for combating the abrupt coolness that often arrives at sunset, as well as for knotting around the abdomen during the day to prevent the chilling otherwise threatened by unusually fast evaporation of perspiration.

Wearing the clothing otherwise open and loose will help maintain the even rate of evaporation necessary for maintenance of normal temperature.

Pockets

All pockets should be kept buttoned, snapped, pinned, or otherwise fastened shut. It also is a good idea, particularly when pushing through thick brush, to check periodically to make sure that pocket tops remain safely closed over contents whose value, if selection has been careful, will increase in proportion to the distance one is away from sources of supply.

If you sleep in your clothes, you will rest more comfortably if you first carefully empty the pockets, keeping the items safely together perhaps in a handkerchief.

Mosquitoes Prefer Blue

Wet clothing is about four times as appealing to mosquitoes as dry. Clothing moist with perspiration attracts at least twice as many of the winged biters as the same garments dampened by rain or dew. Although deer and similar animals, being apparently colorblind, do not seem to notice hues except as varying degrees of brightness, a mosquito has definite preferences, blue being particularly attractive to the pestiferous squadrons.

Jacket

If you can locate a light down jacket that is not too bulky
and which is built ruggedly enough for bush use, you'll have
a particularly adaptable garment for all seasons. One I found
has been comfortable throughout the year in latitudes as far
apart as Alaska and Mexico, and it is light enough to shove
into a game pocket or under the lashings of my dog's pack.
Most of the few such genuine articles on the market, however,
are because of cost and fragility better suited for country club
wear.

Gloves or Mitts

You may want a light pair of leather or woolen gloves to
protect the hands. If warmth is an important factor, woolen
mittens will be more satisfactory, especially:

(1) if they extend high enough to shield the particularly
vulnerable wrists,

(2) and if their tops also fit sufficiently close to exclude
snow and debris which otherwise might necessitate frequent
removals.

If you have had much reason to use mitts in the wilderness,
you have probably found it as suitable as I have to have a slit
made in the palm of one and a knitted flap added to cover
that opening when it is not in use. With such a mitt on the
master hand, one is enabled to bare the fingers quickly whenever this may become expedient, as for example when game
is sighted.

In very cold weather, you may care to add outer mitts.
These may be of some windproof material such as tightly
woven cotton, light and porous enough to maintain a circulation of air adequate to keep perspiration from collecting. An
especially handy technique in this instance, in reasonably open
country, is to join these mitts with a cord long enough to
loop around the neck. Then, protected against loss by the
cord, you can yank either hand bare in an instant with your
teeth.

Chapter 15

Keeping Covered

THAT OUR TWO FEET may one day be our only means of reaching safety there can be no dispute, and if in such a crisis footwear should give out, who will not agree that whenever it may be advantageous other clothing should be sacrificed to protect these vital and vulnerable parts.

Yet numerous lost individuals have been, when found, still well garbed except for long since bare feet actually torn through to the bone in places.

Pieces of heavy cloth can be torn from a mackinaw and, once they are stood upon, drawn up around the ankles and there tied. Strips ripped from a shirt and wound around the legs like puttees, covering the tops of the footwear can be invaluable in protecting the feet from sand and debris in some types of going.

Any time we can no longer keep our feet in reasonably good condition, the best strategy will almost always be to camp and if seeking help to set out distress signs.

Saving What We Have

The worst enemy to which man subjects leather is heat so excessive that it hardens, shrivels, and cracks. Far more outdoor apparel of all types is ruined by attempting to dry it too rapidly than by any other single error, and this is particularly true in the case of footwear. For very often leather becomes too warm when suspended anywhere near the top of a small heated shelter although perhaps twenty feet from a stove.

Whenever leather is dried, the process should be carried out as gradually as possible at as low a temperature as feasible, any mistakes being on the side of conservatism. Better than setting wet shoes near a fire, for example, is wiping them clean and then hanging them where they will be just within the outer influences of gently circulating warm air.

You have probably already found it helpful to stuff wet shoes with something such as dry moss or grass, both to maintain shape and to absorb dampness. A satisfactory way to deal with rubberbottom boots, as it is likely you have also discovered, is to suspend them upside down and to wipe out the moisture accumulated in the feet before putting them back on. Once the leather is dry, a profitable habit is to recondition it by lightly rubbing in a small amount of something such as neat's foot oil.

Water Repellent

Oil driven from animal fat by heat is widely used for greasing footwear to make it more water repellent. Among the better tallows procurable for this purpose in the wilderness are those which can be rendered from the hoofs and feet of animals such as moose, antelope, and mountain goats.

It is not uncommon for individuals to make such garments as stag shirts water resistent by rubbing them with hands dipped in oil of one kind or another, but if intense cold is a threat, such a practice can be dangerous in the extreme and this for two reasons. Grease both directly and indirectly reduces the efficiency of a garment worn for warmth:

(1) by itself conducting body heat rapidly away,

(2) and by filling the inert air spaces in a fabric which otherwise provide most of its insulating characteristics.

Emergency Foot Protection

One way to protect our feet, if soles prove too thin or if disintegrating stockings perhaps worn double and even triple finally give out, is by bedding these extremities in dry grass or dry moss. The wild material chosen must be carefully selected so as to exclude any harsh or irritating matter such as bark or twigs. Footwear should be taken off and such padding painstakingly renewed whenever we feel the advisability of it, a reserve supply perhaps being carried in the pockets for this purpose.

As for innersoles, these may be provided as readily as might be expected by the employment of birchbark and similar substances free for the taking.

Fur and Feathers

The fur of such an easily snared animal as the rabbit is extremely soft but, unfortunately, also so extraordinarily fragile that when used in lieu of something better it needs all possible protection. Rabbit skins tied around the feet like duffels will, if worn alone, last scarcely long enough to justify the effort. Used in conjunction with other materials, say between stockings and boots, the pelt's gentleness can be enjoyed while its fragility is being guarded.

Other skins can be similarly used, generally with the fur turned in toward the foot. More durable bird skins, particularly the breasts of water fowl, are warm and resilient when worn between feet and outer covering. These latter can be improvised if need be from bark or even wood, held on by wide straps or similar bindings. When possible in such an exigency, it is preferable to cushion the feet directly with wool or some other substance that will absorb and dissipate perspiration.

Moccasins

If we have animal skins, we can make moccasins. We can also fashion moccasins from such fabrics as blankets, but under ordinary circumstances these will seldom wear long enough to merit the trouble. Nor are excessively perishable hides worth bothering with for moccasins.

Soft tanned leather provides an easily worked and comfortably light material for moccasin making, but it soon wears

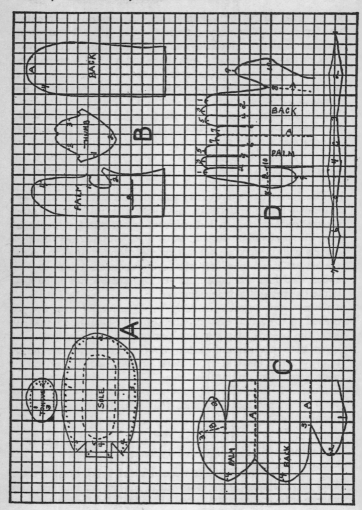

Fig. 42. Patterns for making moccasins, mittens, and gloves.

out in rough or wet going. In such places as the Continental Northwest where this type of foot covering is worn a great deal, the ordinary practice even among aborigines is to protect them from dampness with store rubbers and overshoes.

For a more enduring moccasin that would give the feet stancher protection we would, especially under survival conditions, use as stiff and tough a chunk of hide as possible. When it came to preparing the green skin, we would not take any steps to soften it. Not only would we not tan it, but we'd scrape it only enough to smooth out any irregularities that might hurt the feet. The hair could be left facing inward.

One moccasin pattern which has the virtue of being as practical as it is simple is shown by the following illustration. You will find that you can fit the pattern to your size by standing on the material to be used, or on a more easily manipulated sample, and first drawing an oval around the foot. You will not attempt to trace closely to the ends of the toes probably, preferring no doubt to allow an arc that will provide sufficient room for free movement.

You can then add about three inches all around for the sides of the moccasin. Or if you have plenty of leather, you may want to bring these high around the ankle in two flaps which can be tied by wrapping them with several turns or so of lacing.

We can save ourselves work in the beginning, if such manu-

KEY FOR DRAWINGS

A. Match numbers
B. Match numbers
   a. When joining, pucker to fit.
   b. Sew in stretched elastic if available. Drawstring may be substituted to afford means of tightening.
C. Match numbers
   a. Fold under.
   b. Fold up.
D. Match numbers
   a. Fold under.
   b. Fold up.
   c. Glove gusset (fit in between fingers to allow freedom of action).

facture has not been among our previous pursuits, by making to start with a trial moccasin from as correspondingly thick a piece of fabric as may be available. Two of these can be later used, incidentally, as linings or slippers.

Once the pieces of the moccasin are cut, you'll punch or slit holes around the edges as shown in the drawing. Thongs can easily be made from odd bits of leather by cutting them around and around as later described. These or some other lacing you'll run through the holes so as to join the parts as marked.

How to Make Lacing

A thong or lace can be cut from something such as an old moccasin top or odd piece of rawhide. If we have a sharp knife, one method is to find a smooth log with a branch or stub sticking up that can be used as a guide.

Let us assume, for those who have never tried this way before, that we want a lace one-quarter inch thick. First, let us round any square corners from the leather. Second, let us start the lace, making one or two inches by severing a narrow strip from the main stock.

Fig. 43. Making lacing.

Now comes the mechanics. Using a billet of wood, we tap the knife point-first into the log so that the blade is facing away from us one-fourth of an inch from the projection. We then place the lace between this guide and the knife. Then by pulling the lace and turning the leather, we can cut around and around, manufacturing as long a thong as there is material.

Tanning

Tanning is simple enough, like starting a fire with bow and drill, but as you may be willing to agree it requires considerable work and infinite patience. If we do need leather instead of rawhide, if we have just secured a suitable animal such as a deer, and if we are camped in one place without too much else to occupy us, here is one of the primitive ways to go about the task.

Skin out the animal carefully, taking care to nick and cut the hide no more than necessary. With a sharp knife or similar instrument, working over your knee if you want, remove as much flesh and fat as possible. Then weight the skin down in water for several days, until patches of hair slip out when you give them an easy tug.

Upon retrieving the hide, lay it on a log, the bark of which you have removed if that is necessary for smoothness. Scrape one side and then the other, removing hair and grain. Many consider it best to complete this process in one operation before the hide dries. It can be redampened, however. By driving the point of the longest knife you have into a smooth knot of wood, you can provide an additional hold for manipulating the graining tool with both hands.

When this labor of eradicating hair and grain is completed, the still moist hide may be thoroughly rubbed with a mixture of, for instance, the animal's fat and brains that have been simmered together in equal amounts. The hide is allowed to remain in this state for several days. Then it should be washed as clean as possible. Wring it as well as you can, perhaps by rolling it loosely around two poles that are laying parallel and then turning these in opposite directions.

The skin must then be pulled, rubbed, and stretched while drying if you don't want it to become stiff. If you plan to use it for footwear, however, any rigidity will be a virtue.

The hide may finally be smoked by hanging it well away

from the campfire for a few days, within reach of smoke but not of heat. Or you can make a special smudge with green or rotten wood, taking the same precautions regarding warmth. The sweet oily fumes produced by birch achieve a particularly pleasing effect.

Rawhide

Rawhide is prepared more easily. You can dry the green skin in the shade, at odd moments scraping the flesh side as clean as possible with any dull instrument such as a piece of rock or bone flattened on one side. The skin may be conveniently held by stretching across the knee that portion that is being worked, or like many of us you may prefer to leave it tacked or pegged to some smooth surface where hungry birds will in all probability aid your efforts.

If you want the rawhide to be soft, you will probably have to wet the flesh side, allow it to dry, and then rescrape the skin, doing this as many times as may be necessary until the hide is satisfactorily pliable.

Care must be taken not to dampen the other side if retention of hair or fur is desired. If this is too long, it may be clipped. If you want it off entirely, that can be easily enough accomplished when the pelt is first secured by wetting the coat until it starts to slip, whereupon you can scrape it off in great clumps.

Repairs

If we pocket only as large a repair kit as can be carried in a screw top plastic container about the size of a 12-gauge shotgun shell, we can solve as they arise a multitude of minor clothing problems. Such a kit may well contain several needles of assorted sizes, a few lengths of thread rolled on bits of cardboard, safety pins, and any odds and ends we may care to tuck in such as nylon fish line, wire, rubber bands, snaps, and perhaps several assorted copper rivets.

Buttons, certainly, will be no problem anywhere. A short bone or piece of wood, attached by the middle, will serve. So will a bit of leather such as may be cut from the end of a belt.

The dogbane which grows in sandy places is among the wild growths, discoverable by experimentation, which have furnished many a frequenter of the farther places with thread. Thin strips of dried rawhide are generally handier for ordinary wilderness use, however. Strong thread can be made from fibers raveled from clothing, especially by twisting and winding them as described under the subject of improvising fish lines. If we secure meat to eat, we will also have at our disposal the sinews of the animal.

Keeping Warm With Feathers

When one is short of warm clothing in the wilderness, the down and feathers of any birds that can be secured should be saved for warmth. If we have no better way of utilizing these, we can merely shove them beneath the clothing. Birds may also be skinned and the plumage made into crude garments, preferably by basting it to some garment that can be worn beneath regular garb.

Hair of the various members of the deer family has considerable insulating worth. It may be distributed beneath the clothing, or a skin may be scraped as clean as possible, dried, and worn. Vegetable substances such as grass, leaves, and dry moss stuffed within the clothes will also afford a great deal of warmth.

Furs

The more perishable furs are under survival conditions best used for warmth when sandwiched within protective coverings. One way that northern Indians accomplish this today is by covering a piece of burlap or other material with skins of the varying hare, overlapping them like shingles and sewing them in place. The layer is usually later covered with a second section of fabric to form a blanket.

Another method, also still employed beneath the Northern Lights, is commenced by cutting and sewing the skins together in long ribbons. These strips are sometimes loosely woven as is, while on other occasions they are first given body by being wound flatly around and around a leather thong which the maker may know as babiche or shaganappie. In either event, the final slackly interlaced robe is commonly basted between two outer coverings, on the weather side a husky section of water repellent canvas perhaps and on the other a thin woolen blanket.

Emergency Waterproofs

We can even improvise emergency waterproofs. Large sections of birchbark, held in place by thrusting them under outer clothing, will turn considerable water.

Crude bark garments are sometimes put together. A thread made by Indians particularly for use in sewing birchbark is prepared by simmering in water the fine roots of the spruce tree. Punches are used instead of needles. The root is pulled through the cut and fastened to itself by a cross-stitch. Spruce gum, incidentally, is often relied upon for sealing bark seams when this is adjudged necessary.

Some aborigines make waterproof garments by opening the dried intestines of large animals and sewing the strips together vertically with sinew.

PART THREE

ORIENTATION

"If for any reason you leave emergency
camp, even if only for a short period,
leave a note in an obvious place
stating in detail your plans and where
you are going."

—*Hudson's Bay Company*

Chapter 16

Staying Found

JUST AS COLD is actually the lack of heat, and as what we know as darkness is no more than the absence of light, so is getting lost an entirely negative state of affairs. We become lost not because of anything we do, but because of what we leave undone.

It is when we realize this that all the mysteries imputed to the procedure of finding one's way through wilderness vanish, and in their place appears a positive and ever intriguing problem of distances and angles. For there is just one method to keep from getting lost, and that is to stay found.

We stay found by knowing approximately where we are every moment, nor is this as complicated as it may at first seem, for any one of us can keep track of his whereabouts by means of a map, compass, and pencil. Every ten or fifteen minutes, or whenever direction is changed, will not in the beginning be too often to bring that map up to date. Suppose we do not have a map? Then we draw one as we go.

The sagest old sourdough uses the same system, whether he realizes it or not. His map is in his mind, that's all. Sun, stars, prevailing wind, vegetation, landmarks, and numerous other natural factors may be the veteran woodsman's compass— under, it should be well noted, favorable conditions.

By timing ourselves or by otherwise measuring distances,

and by making either a written or mental record of all angles of travel, we get so that we can always tell just about how far away in what direction lies the spot from which we started.

What About Following Streams?

The more you and I learn about the wilderness, the more poignantly do we realize that no way of thinking or doing, however venerable, can be trusted without proof. Although innumerable widely accepted opinions sound reasonable enough in theory, too many of these have the often fatal tendency of not working out in practice.

An example is the counsel that following a stream downhill will eventually lead us back to civilization. In well settled country it will, usually, if we take the sometimes unmentioned precaution of keeping to the higher sides of any swamps. In a reasonably populous area it will, ordinarily, if we can keep going long enough through the comparatively heavy growth and downfall which characterize watercourses.

In real wilderness, particularly under the stresses imposed by emergency conditions either real or imagined, following a strange stream with any assurance is something else again. Nor is keeping well to one side so as to have easier walking, and cutting back often enough to maintain contact, the solution.

For suppose we manage to detour impassable gorges? Suppose we are successful in circumventing morasses and marshlands? Suppose we can continue to twist and batter our way perhaps a dozen exhausting miles through alder and willow for every mile gained? The flow may very well end in an isolated pond even farther back of beyond.

Who Should Carry a Compass?

Even the most experienced frontiersman does well to carry a compass, as well as matches, whenever in the bush if only to save time and energy. For instance, you and I are on a Gaspe Peninsula knoll. The sun has set. We can glimpse smoke curling up a mile away from the tents where all day

Vena has had a mulligan simmering. Heading directly there in the straightest possible line can mean the difference between arriving easily and safely during the remaining daylight and taking the needless chance of getting a dead branch in the eye.

So we sight over a compass. The tents lie exactly south by the needle. Once we've dropped down to the flat, we're in small thick spruce so dense that some of the time we have to get down and crawl. We can not see far enough ahead to line up a straight route without a lot of time-consuming care, but checking the compass occasionally assures our keeping headed in the shortest direction.

Or we're on the other side of the continent, atop a Yukon mountain. A cloud swirls about us, blotting out all landmarks. Camp, we've ascertained during the climb, lies east down what is the only safe slope. The weather is thick by now. Which way is east? If we have a compass, we neither have to wait on this exposed peak for the atmosphere to clear, nor need we risk any undue or unnecessarily dangerous scrambling.

How Tenderfeet can be Superior to Natives

What is often regarded as a natural sense of direction is instead almost always the result of either (a) acquired skill apparently so effortless as to appear instinctive, or (b) familiarity with the surroundings.

The settler who lives on the edge of a clearing can be expected to become as closely acquainted with the woods surrounding as the city boy with the streets of his own neighborhood. The ruralist in a strange countryside and the urbanite in an unfamiliar metropolis will if depending solely on familiarity both become lost.

Knowledge of locality becomes less and less valuable the farther we travel, for few of us can make a very long journey without leaving the region we know. This is a major reason why explorers the world over have been repeatedly plagued by the desertions of aborigine guides. Natives, although they may have spent their entire existence in primitive places, and in fact to an important extent because of the psychological handicaps imposed by these very limitations, have always been in the main characteristically terrified to venture very far beyond the particular area each has come to know.

The greenest tenderfoot among us who learns and uses even the small amount of wilderness lore set forth in this book will be able to find his way as surely in one forest as in another.

The Essentials of Getting Back

If camp lies against some long and easily followed landmark, such as a sub-arctic river with a smooth hard shore, returning there after a day afield can be practically foolproof. It is in such a place that an experienced man will whenever possible be careful to locate his camp, for he will still be able

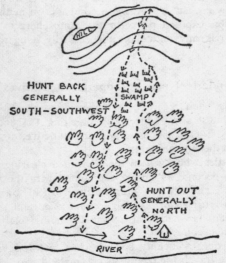

FIG. 44. Camp Lies East.

to find it although the weather becomes stormy and the night black. Where I've lived for some years in the still largely unmapped and unexplored primitiveness of northern British

Columbia, becoming lost could be serious in the extreme. We could walk from our homesite for veritably hundreds of miles and never cross a road nor see the most meager sign of habitation. It would very likely be weeks, furthermore, before anyone even realized we were missing.

That would have concerned us a lot more than it actually did, particularly at first, if it were not for the fact that the Peace River cuts from west to east through these mountains and foothills. Our home in the woods is on the sunny north bank. Any time we keep on traveling south while on this side we're bound to reach the great waterway. If we happen to be on the south shore instead, it's merely a matter of reversing the direction and heading north.

After even the roughest general reckoning, therefore, we'd be halted by the Peace River and guided by it to our log home. The country alters sufficiently, becoming more precipitous upstream and leveling to eventual plains toward the east, so that at worst we'd then have no excuse for proceeding in the wrong direction for very far.

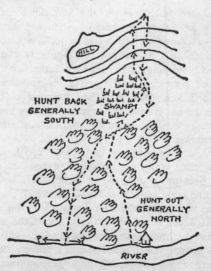

HILL

HUNT BACK
GENERALLY
SOUTH

SWAMP

HUNT OUT
GENERALLY
NORTH

RIVER

FIG. 45. Which way is camp?

Why Experts Bear to One Side

The proceeding is admittedly a broad example, for all of us will generally want to keep sufficient track of our whereabouts to be able to intersect a broadside such as a road or river within a reasonable distance of the spot desired. The question of which way then to turn should not ordinarily be left to chance, however.

Coming upon an unmarked destination directly involves such a disproportionate percentage of chance that rarely is it wise even to attempt it. Unless there are guiding factors such as landmarks on which we can rely, the most expert technique by far is to bear definitely to one particular side of the target.

Then upon reaching the trail, shore, or whatever the lateral may be, we will know at once which way to follow it; knowledge that can save time, energy, and therefore one day perhaps life itself.

Picking Up Trail Going Away

Somewhat more difficult is picking up a dead end trail that somewhere ahead comes into being by running directly away from us. By adapting the lore we have just been considering, however, this problem we can also solve handily and certainly.

We are in a level pine forest, let us assume for the sake of interest. Earlier we came to the end of a long fire lane that slashes due north and south. For three hours since then we've continued to hike northward by compass, the day being cloudy and the country more enhanced by animals and singing birds than by landmarks.

We have boiled the noonday kettle, you and I, and now it is the halfway time when we should head back to camp. We would prefer because of distance to return there by the faster going of the fire lane. How should we proceed?

Do we hike back southward by compass at the same pace with the idea of rejoining the trail in about the same three hours? The flaw in that procedure, we realize, is that straight lines are only a manner of speaking in ordinary bush travel. The most that we will reasonably be able to count on in that

respect is that variations will roughly balance one another if
by mark or compass we compensate for drift and keep headed
in the same general direction.

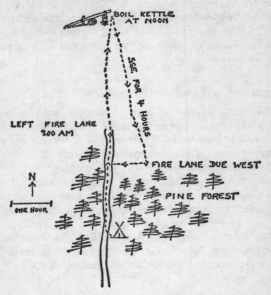

FIG. 46. Picking up trail going away.

But suppose we do travel south for three hours, and then
for one more hour, at the same pace we've been walking all
day? Unless we have already encountered the lane by that
time, we may be as sure as one is of anything that the lane
now lies either west or east of us.

What at that hypothetical point would be the desirable procedure? To try going due west, say, for up to fifteen minutes,
with the knowledge that if we hadn't cut the lane by that time,
we should cross it within a half-hour by hiking back due
east? Or to begin zigzagging methodically southeast and southwest, increasing these lines until the lane is reached?

All such approaches, you rightly decided, leave a great deal unnecessarily to chance. Percentages favor our reaching the trail with less time and bother by aiming at it from one definite side. So we don't proceed due south at all. Instead, because for example the going is somewhat more open that way, we choose to bear slightly east of due south. Then after traveling for the same safe four hours, we can swing west with the assurance that the fire lane lies broadside a short way off in that direction.

Returning to a Blind Camp

Now let us suppose that a small party of us have pitched our tents beside a spring in flat dense wilderness where there are no roads or landmarks. Everyone has to leave camp separately each day to carry on prospecting operations. How do we all find our respective ways back each evening?

The reasonable solution will be to make a mark at which to aim. One way to do this is by blazing four lines, each perhaps a mile long depending on the circumstances, north, east, south, and west from camp. To save time that would later be wasted in following any of these radii in the wrong direction, some informative system can be used such as cutting the higher blaze on each tree on the side nearer camp.

Maps

Maps, be they but memorized before or during a journey or delineated during the progress thereof, are necessities for intelligent wilderness travel. It is sound procedure, for this reason, to study whenever possible during the course of any trip maps of the area and to compare them to what we can see so as to obtain at least a general picture of the vicinity.

There are maps available to the passengers of most commercial planes, for example, or a supply can be picked up at terminals. Seeing where we are makes any flight more enjoyable for most of us, and even rough knowledge of this sort may help us to decide more surely what to do and perhaps where to head in case of a forced landing under circumstances in which decisions can be vital.

Making Sure of Topographical Facts

If we don't have time to procure a map or the opportunity to copy one before taking to the bush, some native can often be found who will take pleasure in sketching a practical chart of the countryside. It is a profitable habit in any event to ask old habitants to correct and supplement local maps if we are in extreme wilderness where the hardest working and most conscientious surveyor can do only a sketchy job in the few weeks when it is possible for him to hack, blaze, perspire, and swat his way through the bush.

In any event, we should either be sure of the basic topographical facts, or we should not depend on them. Skid, tote, and other roads come to dead ends. Prominent ridges melt into level country. Even large streams disappear underground, sometimes for miles at a time.

Where to Get Maps

Good maps are in general extraordinarily easy to obtain. Even the small-scale maps distributed free by gasoline stations give enough of a general picture to enable a lot more individuals to go into the woods from parked automobiles and to find their ways safely back again than, as you may have observed, manage to accomplish this feat.

Sectional maps, particularly those governmental publications which are sold below cost, are inexpensive in the extreme. Furthermore, most suppliers will furnish upon request free detailed lists of exactly what they have available.

Maps of these portions of the United States east of the Mississippi River may be secured from the U. S. Geological Survey, Washington, D. C. For maps of areas west of the Mississippi, contact the U. S. Geological Survey, Federal Center, Denver, Colorado.

For maps of national forest areas, write the Forest Service, Department of Agriculture, Washington, D. C. Maps of the Great Lakes and connecting waters may be obtained from the U. S. Lake Survey, Federal Building, Detroit, Michigan.

Canadian maps may be secured from provincial publicity

offices located in the various province capitols, from the Government Travel Bureau in Ottawa, and from the Map Distribution Office, Department of Mines and Technical Surveys, which is also located in Ottawa, Ontario.

For governmental maps of Mexico, write: Direccion de Geografia y Meteorologia, Tacusaya, D. F., Mexico. Two private sources for foreign maps are: The National Geographical Society, 16th and M Streets, Washington, D. C.; and the International Map Company, 90 West Street, New York, N. Y.

Why Contour Maps are Preferable

Contour maps when available are by far the most valuable for wilderness use, indicating as they do valleys, canyons, mountains, and other such geographical features in terms of elevations. Consulting such a map in strange country can save one an exhausting amount of unnecessary climbing, descending, and then scaling again.

Traveling by compass in a straight line is, even when possible, often no more advisable than might be expected. In mountains, for example, we soon learn that on more than one occasion both time and strength can be conserved by circling several miles along an open ridge instead of striking a small fraction of that distance straight across a deep ravine to the same destination.

Chapter 17

Knowing Where You Are

IT ISN'T SO MUCH a question of whether or not we can get along without a compass. That most of us can learn to do, for even in the strangest surroundings there are numerous recognizable signs that indicate direction, and some of these are more accurate than the wavering magnetized needle. But traveling through unmarked places without a compass is in the same unnecessarily arduous category as lighting a fire without matches.

Making a Temporary Compass

The compass—which along with gunpowder was one of the wonders brought from the Orient to Europe nearly seven centuries ago by Marco Polo—was, some four thousand years earlier, a chunk of magnetic iron ore suspended by a rawhide lace. Today the most simple compass is a magnetized needle mounted on a pivot so that it can rotate freely.

We can make a temporary compass, in fact, by first stroking an ordinary needle in a single direction with a piece of silk or with the pocket magnet we may have with us if prospecting. The next step will be to place the thus magnetized needle so that it will be free to turn. This we can accomplish a little more easily than otherwise if now we rub the needle with oil, the small amount that can be collected by passing a thumb and forefinger over the nose and forehead being sufficient.

Then let us take two thin bits of grass, or some other fiber, and double them to form two loops in which to suspend the needle. Holding it thus, let us lower it carefully into still water such as a tiny pool trapped by a stump or rock. If we are careful, the top of the water will bend noticeably under the needle but the surface tension will still float it. The support may then be cautiously removed.

The floating needle, once freed, will turn until it is aligned with the north and south magnetic poles unless, as is the case with any compass, some metal is near enough to distract it. If we have stroked the needle from the head to the tip, the head will point north.

North Pole or Magnetic Pole

Compasses as you already know do not point true north toward the North Pole unless it be by chance, for they are governed instead by the so-called Magnetic Pole. This magnetic field, which is energized by the earth's whirling on its axis, is situated some 1400 miles below the North Pole near where the shallow Northwest Passage winds icily above Hudson Bay.

Even the compass line to the Magnetic Pole is not constant, inasmuch as this magnetic center is all the time drifting. For all ordinary purposes of determining direction, however, a small plain compass can be used with sufficient accuracy. The only correction usually necessary is to allow for the general declination in a particular section so as to read more exactly the maps of that area.

Compass Declination

Compass declination is the difference, if any, between true north and magnetic north. This variance is customarily indicated on most local maps.

The compass points due north in the United States and Canada only in a narrow strip, which passes through the

Great Lakes, where the North and Magnetic Poles happen to be in line. In parts of Maine, the indicator trembles to a rest twenty-five degrees west of north. At the other side of the continent in British Columbia, the angle is as great in an easterly direction.

So as to make this record a little more complete, let us review how very simple a matter compass correction for map reading is. Suppose we are scouting over the boulder-studded hills above Ensenada in Baja California. The compass declination where we are is about 14° east of north. Our compass, in other words, here points 14° too far east.

Watching out for cacti, we spread our map before us on the semi-arid ground. An arrow marked N verifies that north is at the top of the chart, which unless otherwise indicated is the case with most maps; the bottom then being south, the right side east, and the left side west. We move the map until the printed arrow, or until one side of the upright rectangular sheet if there is no such mark, points 14° west of compass north. For all practical purposes, we can now read the map in terms of the countryside about us.

Perhaps on the map we have there is a second arrow marked M to indicate magnetic north. All we have to do in this case is move the map until this second arrow and our compass needle both head in the same direction.

Compass Degrees

All circles no matter what their size are divided into 360 degrees, and so it is with the compass dial where these degrees may perhaps be most easily visualized as 360 possible routes fanning out like wheel spokes from wherever we happen to be. Compass degrees are customarily numbered in a clockwise direction starting at north.

East is one-fourth of the way around the compass dial. East in terms of degree is, as can be seen, one-fourth of 360° which is 90°. The distance between each of the four cardinal points—north, east, south, and west—is the same 90°. South is therefore often designated as 180° and west as 270°.

Northeast is halfway between north and east. Northeast in

terms of degrees is, then, half of 90° which is 45°. Half of that again, or 22.5°, is north-northeast.

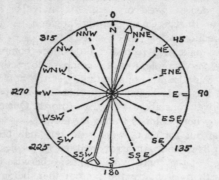

FIG. 47. Compass dial.

Compass Points

We usually learn while youngsters that when by standard time we stand facing the sun at noon, south is directly in front of us and north is at our back. And if we are to lift our arms straight up from our sides to shoulder height, our left hand will point east and our right hand will point west.

Halfway between north and east is called, logically, northeast. The other corresponding points are similarly determined and named; southeast, southwest, and northwest.

There will be occasions when we will want to figure direction even more finely. This we can do by using the divisions halfway between each of the already considered eight points. These additional eight points are named with equal logic. Halfway between north and northeast is north-northeast. Halfway between northeast and east? East-northeast. Each of the four cardinal points always comes first. Halfway between south and southwest is, therefore, south-southwest.

What Kind of Compass to Buy

It is possible my assertion that any compass carried for ordinary wilderness use should have a luminous indicator will be questioned, but not, I believe, by anyone who has been forced to sacrifice time and increasingly precious matches to maintain a compass course at night.

It is also no more than reasonable to expect any compass we buy to be rugged enough to stand up under rough usage, and to have some provision so that it can be attached securely to the person.

The handiest and altogether most practical compass I've personally found for day by day travel in strange wilderness is the small luminous Marble's Pin-On Compass. This fastens, when desired, to the outside of the clothing where it is constantly available as is for quick examination, and the fact that the entire dial moves makes this consultation even easier.

Do You Need a Second Compass?

Not a few of us carry a second compass, and the practice is a sound one, for even if you or I never do lose or damage the first, the bulge of a spare fastened safely in a pocket is ever reassuring.

Many can also testify to being plagued by the doubt that the compass on which they are relying may be no longer in order, and an auxiliary will be welcomed at such moments for checking purposes. If we ever do this, let us:

(1) place or hold the two compasses level,

(2) keep them well away from each other and from any metallic objects, and

(3) make sure that the indicator of each is swinging freely on its pivot. If there should be any marked discrepancy, let us go by the compass whose needle oscillates most freely in gradually narrowing arcs before quivering to a stop.

Hours Not Miles

The special value of a watch in the wilderness has to do with our measuring distance in the farther places less often by miles than by time. If we walk three hours along a beach, to give an example, we may not be sure if we have traversed six miles or nine miles. But we can be certain that if we return over the same route at about the same pace, a similar three hours will bring us close to our starting point.

Miles as such mean little in ordinary backwoods travel, for although a trail may proceed through level open country, it may as readily dip and twist down coulees and through old burns.

Suppose you ask a trapper as I did once, "How far is it along this blaze to the mine road?"

His laconic reply, "Six miles," may not give any realistic indication of what lies ahead. If instead he says, "Oh, I reckon six hours if you keep hustling," you also will probably inquire if there isn't some easier approach.

Using Watch as Compass

A watch used as a makeshift compass in the United States and Canada can be relied upon to be true within eight degrees, depending upon where we happen to be in any of the 15°-wide time zones. Three factors are prerequisites:

(a) the sun must be shining brightly enough to throw a shadow,

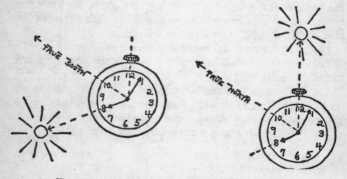

FIG. 48. Telling direction by watch and sun.

(b) the timepiece must be accurately set,
(c) it must show the local standard Greenwich time.
The watch we lay face up with the hour hand pointing di-

rectly toward the sun. This can be checked by our holding a twig or pine needle upright at the edge of the dial, whereupon it should angle a shadow directly along this shorter hand.

South will then lie midway along the smaller arc between the hour hand and twelve o'clock. If such a procedure is carried out at eight o'clock in the morning, therefore, a line drawn from the center of the watch outward through the numeral ten will point south.

Setting Watch by Compass

By reversing the principle of using a watch to ascertain direction, we can tell time by the use of a compass. Whereas previously the timepiece had to be accurate, now it is the compass that has to be read exactly, and for this purpose local magnetic variations must be taken into account.

If we are in the United States or Canada and want to set a watch, let us ascertain by compass which way is due south. Then using a shadow to help us keep the hour hand of the watch pointed at the sun, let us turn the hour hand until south lies midway along the shorter arc between it and the numeral twelve. The watch will then be set to within a few minutes of the correct local standard time.

If we are in the bush with a watch but no compass, we can still proceed in the above manner by previously lining up two stakes so that they point toward the North Star. Such a line will run almost exactly north and south.

Determining Direction by Sun Alone

Suppose we've no watch. We've no compass. It's morning. The sun is shining. We want to know precisely where *south* is.

Drive a short pole into the ground. Observe how long a shadow the pole casts. Loop a string, lace, piece of straw, or something similar around the pole. Keep this taut and, holding it at the desired length to a sharp stick draw an arc that exactly touches the end of the shadow. Mark this point with a stake.

The shadow of the pole will keep shortening until noon, at which time it'll commence lengthening. Watch until it once more meets the arc. Mark that spot with a second stake.

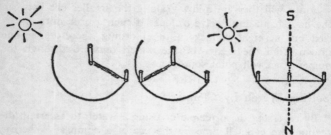

FIG. 49. Telling exact direction by sun.

A line connecting the center with a point halfway between the first and second stakes will point due *south*.

Unless we use some such device, it is difficult except after long experience or very painstaking attention to do more than estimate direction by the sun alone. The sun rises in the east, we are told. It sets in the west, we learn.

The trouble is that the sun keeps rising and setting in widely different positions, appearing exactly in the east and disappearing truly in the west only two days each year. These are known as the equinox and fall approximately on March 21 and September 23. Even on these two annual occasions, when the sun's center crosses the equator and when night and day are therefore both twelve hours long, true east and west can be determined with certainty only over flat areas.

Polaris

There is no more reliable way to pinpoint north if the North Star is visible than by consulting this orb known as Polaris. The bright polestar seems to the naked eye to be by itself in the heavens. It is most easily located by following an imaginary line up through the two stars that form the outer edge of the big dipper.

Polaris is such an infallible signpost that if we are close to anyone who does not already know its whereabouts well, we may want to show that individual with the least possible delay

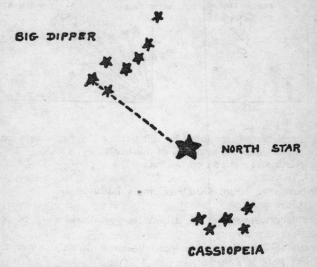

Fig. 50. Locating the North Star by means of the "Pointers" of the Big Dipper.

how always to recognize it. Not only can such knowledge be of help on inestimable occasions when there may be a doubt about direction, but on times innumerable it has saved lives, and the next life so involved may be that of someone especially important to us.

Longitude and Latitude

Longitude, depicted by the vertical lines running from pole to pole on maps is represented either by degrees or by time, both reckoned from Greenwich, England. Latitude, marked by the horizontal lines parallel to the equator, can be determined in North America by observing the North Star, knowledge that for someone shipwrecked or down in a plane disaster may greatly increase his chances of reaching safety.

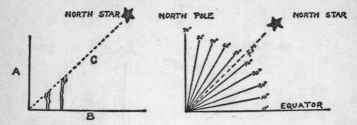

A. Weighted string.
B. Level can be established by still water or by right angle from plumb line, such as corner of this book.
C. North Star sighted over two stakes.

FIG. 51. Determining Latitude.

This determination of latitude is possible because of two factors:

(a) the North Star is located almost directly above the North Pole at a 90° angle,

(b) at the equator the North Star lies straight ahead on the horizon at 0°.

If we are halfway between the North Pole and Equator on the 45th parallel, we will therefore find upon sighting the North Star that it lies almost exactly at a 45° angle from us.

At whatever degree angle the North Star when visible lies away from us, that is within a single degree also the degree of latitude. The diagram shows a practical way of making this estimation which, if only makeshift devices are at hand, can be but an approximation.

M or W

Most of us know that, depending on what time we look at them, the five stars known as Cassiopeia appear either as an M or a W. This northern constellation is always on the opposite side of the North Star from the Big Dipper and about the same distance away. By memorizing the relationship between Cassiopeia and the North Star, we can use the former for finding north when the Big Dipper is not visible.

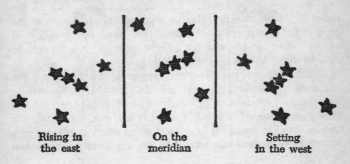

| Rising in the east | On the meridian | Setting in the west |

FIG. 52. Three positions of Orion.

Direction by Any Star

Because of the way the earth is continually revolving, stars seems to swing from east to west in great arcs, forming the white streaks that puzzle some first looking at time-exposure pictures of the night sky. The way in which any star seems to

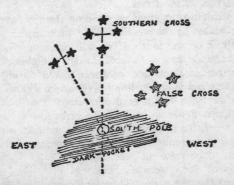

FIG. 53. Southern Hemisphere where North Star is not visible.

move can furnish us, therefore, with a general idea of direction.

We have to take first of all a sight, for the movement is too gradual to detect just by glancing at the heavens. We will need two fixed points over which to watch, and these may be the sights of a stationary rifle, or two stakes driven into the ground for the purpose and their tops lined up carefully. If we will so observe a star for several minutes, it will seem to rise, to move to one side or the other, or to sink.

If the star we are observing seems to be lifting in the heavens, we are looking approximately east. If it appears to be falling, it is situated generally west of us. If the star has the appearance of looping flatly toward our right, we are facing roughly south. If it gives the impression of swinging rather flatly toward our left, then we are heading just about north.

Other Ways to Tell Direction

Moss does grow thickest on the shadiest side of the tree. If a particular tree happens to be in the open where the sun can reach it unimpeded throughout the day, the shadiest side will be north. Also to be taken into consideration is the fact, however, that certain growths resembling moss thrive best on the sunniest portion of the trunk.

The growth rings exposed in standing stumps have a tendency to be widest on the sunniest side which, under ideal conditions, will be on the south. If we will examine a number of such trunks and take into account the influence of such natural factors as slope and probable shade during growth, we can make a rough approximation of where south is located.

Another valuable sign if read correctly is that indicated by downfall. Trees generally fall in the direction of the strong prevailing wind. Such things as freak storms and wind deviations caused by mountains and canyons sometimes give what would seem to be false pictures, however.

The tops of such trees as hemlocks and pines naturally point toward the rising sun. They lean generally east, that is, unless the wind turns them in another direction.

Sand dunes and snowdrifts build up in such a way that they are narrower and lower to windward. The phenomenon is indicative, therefore, if we know from what direction the wind was blowing when the drift was formed. This can usually be determined by a combination of signs, but just as usually does it require calm experience and cool confidence.

Growth also relates its own story, being larger and therefore more open on a north slope, and smaller and consequently denser along a southern exposure. But when in the absence of handier means such as a compass we travel by North Star or by sun, we do not have to do a great deal of averaging and rationalizing.

Chapter 18

Afoot In Big Country

WE HAVE LEARNED how to tell direction by consulting various natural signs, and the way to keep positive track of our whereabouts, and if suddenly plummeted into strange wilderness as by a crashing plane how to find out in what part of the continent we may be. But much as our enjoyment and awareness have been enhanced by this growing knowledge, more remains to be considered that will open the forest aisles to us even more widely.

How to Stay on A Trail

We soon discover that although it is easy to stray from the ordinary bush trail, getting back on such a course can be difficult in the extreme, and that the important and sometimes mortal factor is not to lose the new starting point. Often some landmark, such as an oddly shaped tree, is nearby which we can use as a pivot while methodically searching in widening circles.

If there is no such signpost, a safer way to hunt will be in straight lines from and back to this new beginning point; breaking limbs, cutting blazes, and making any other necessary marks by which to return, all the time checking to make sure the back trail is evident.

This laborious method can also be used by a lost man particularly under conditions where the stakes may be so considerable that every possible precaution against failure should be taken, for ordinarily when one first discovers he is not sure of his whereabouts, he is not very far out of the way.

Ways to Follow Blazes

Staying on an old spotted trail is often tricky unless we pay the closest attention to what are blazes and what instead may be patches where bark has peeled, abrasions made by falling timber, and areas gnawed by such animals as moose and bear.

The apparent blaze can be examined both by touch and by sight for flatness and for other characteristics of human manufacture. Most trails are spotted both going and coming, and one simple way to determine whether or not a mark is a blaze is to check the opposite side of the tree to see if a chip has been cut out of that also.

When one is traveling by the dimness of night, the surest way to authenticate a blaze is by feeling it, and if there is the slightest doubt, this we should do. One telltale clue is the little flap sometimes left at the bottom of the spot where the edge of the ax or knife has driven into the bark but has not entirely disengaged it.

Fire often makes a spotted trail difficult although not impossible to follow. Unless the trees are badly charred, some impression of enough marks generally remain.

If a trail seems to have stopped, the safest procedure is to mark where we are at the moment. Not losing track of that place, let us return as directly as possible to the last blaze of which we're sure. Then by looking back down the blazed trail in the direction from which we have come, we can usually line up how it should and probably does continue. The difficulty immediately ahead may be that a tree has fallen. By figuring where any trail would most reasonably have gone, we will be able in most cases to ascertain where it actually does go.

Night Travel

Night travel is usually inadvisable. One will generally do better under a multitude of circumstances to stop about an hour before darkness, get comfortable for the night, turn in early, and then arise in time to hit the trail again as soon as there is sufficient light.

Desert travel in hot weather is, as noted elsewhere, an exception. Here, particularly if one is short of water, his best deal will be to keep as cool and as quiet as possible during the heat of the day. If no shade is otherwise available, it will usually be worthwhile to scoop out a narrow trench in which to lie. To exclude as much heat as possible, the slit if on a flat should align itself with the rising and setting sun, so that during midday it will be as nearly at right angles as possible to the blazing rays.

The Values of Game Trails

The intriguing skeins of trails worn by the feet of passing animals often make wilderness travel easier, as when we are looking for a gradual way down from some height. If we are trying to hold a certain direction, however, the safest general rule is to follow a game track only as far as it seems to be heading generally where we want to go.

It will be noticed in swampy country that occasionally we will begin to encounter one game trail after another before reaching a muskeg or morass. These are made by animals seeking to avoid the wet places and to keep to easier going. In dry country, such deeply worn ruts often indicate the more welcome nearness of drinking water.

How Small Streams Can Be Deceiving

Using small streams as landmarks in strange country should be only part of one's procedure of orientation. Brooks loop around so much, for example, that when one does encounter the rill for which he has been looking, he may be thrown off by its seeming to flow in the wrong direction. Or a similar stream that runs into the first can be deceiving.

Particularly confusing is the good sized brook which occasionally disappears underground. If one is following it, this phenomenon is simple enough to allow for. But if one is depending on cutting such a stream, he may walk right over it and not be the wiser. The safest rule, then, is not to depend on topography unless one is sure of it.

What About Watersheds?

A general way to keep track of one's whereabouts in big country is by watersheds. This is not a practice to pursue lightly; however, for flowages starting only a few feet apart can and often do end up several thousand miles from each other.

You're camped on a large river into which, as far as you know, all nearby streams drain. One day you don't even hunt as high as usual. You cross a low saddle. It may be that all the water on the other side of this gradient trickles eventually into a brook which has no connection with the river. So if you have fallen into the habit of just following some stream back down each day until it leads you to a recognizable part of the river, you may become seriously confused by attempting this now. Where such divisions are apt to be extremely abrupt are, of course, in mountainous regions.

Chapter 19

Camping And Signaling

"IF GREEN BOUGHS are available, cut plenty," the Hudson's Bay Company advises, "as when burning they make a lot of smoke and a good signal."

Very often the best plan of procedure to adopt when lost or stranded is to stay where we are; moving about as little as possible especially if food is scarce, improvising the easiest shelter if one is advisable for dryness and warmth, and setting about in the most effective ways available trying to attract aid.

When a human being afoot first realizes that he is not sure of his whereabouts, he is ordinarily not so far out of the way that he can not be located—or if need be can not relocate himself—within a safe time.

The trouble very often develops when a lost man keeps blundering along, usually to his own detriment and to the increased confusion of searchers. Too many times he walks entirely out of an area, exhausts himself, and with his last remaining strength instinctively crawls into some dark nook where his bones may not be found for years.

Stay With Aeroplane

"Except under extenuating circumstances when it is obviously only a very short distance to a frequented route or populated area, and there is a negligible chance of any individual becoming lost," Hudson's Bay Company emergency instruction specify, "always stay near the aeroplane. It is much easier to locate an aeroplane that may have been forced down in Northern Canada than an individual walking through the North."

If for any reason whatsoever one goes away from a downed aircraft even for a short period, he owes it to himself and searchers to leave a note in an obvious place stating in detail his plans and where he is going.

A plane that has crashed or been forced to land will be easier to spot if brightly hued and highly reflecting objects are placed on and about it. The Hudson's Bay Company has found it efficacious to remove cowl panels and to place them with their unpainted surfaces upward to act as reflectors.

Colored wing covers, the nearly three century old trading combine had determined, make it easier to locate down aeroplanes from the air. All such items, as well as the aircraft itself, should manifestly be kept clear of snow, frost, and debris.

When flying over isolated areas, especially in a private plane, it is no more than a conservative precaution to have along clothing and particularly footwear that will enable one to fend for himself in the event of a forced landing.

In such an emergency, it is often possible to become generally familiar with the terrain while still air-borne. To a more limited extent this is often feasible even after bailing out, an important factor then being to establish if possible a line to the wrecked plane if only because of its wealth of usually actual and, even after fire, certainly potential survival equipment.

In case of an impending crash landing, what can be all important is to be braced at the moment of severest impact and not to relax at what may be an initial minor shock caused by the tail's touching. Actual continuous bracing must not be started more than a couple of minutes too soon, or faltering muscles will be unable to maintain their tension. A major danger in many instances is that of the head's being snapped disastrously forward. One precaution is to swath the head in coats and in any other protective material that may be available. Another precaution, in the absence of belted seats, is to sit with the back toward the front and with the head held down by firmly clasped hands. Urination is advised to help lower the chances of internal injury.

Signal Fires

A fire, in addition to its warmth and good fellowship, makes one of the better signals, and in fact if we are in any of the numerous areas where regular watches are being maintained from towers and observation planes, we will in an emergency often have only to kindle a blaze to attract necessary help.

One way to send up the smoke that will make a conflagration most conspicuous during daylight is by throwing evergreen boughs into a hot fire. Black smoke can be obtained, too, with oil from a wrecked plane or disabled outboard motor. This is one reason why in cold country the sump oil may well be drained off before congealing, while the plane engine is still warm. Not only does this make a hot fire, particularly when mixed with gasoline, but poured on a hearty blaze it rolls up a tremendous surge of black fumes.

Water will give a white smoke, although as everyone realizes too much dampness will drastically quell and even extinguish the fire. A long lasting smudge can be built, however, by covering hot coals with humid green foliage, wet dead leaves, slowly burning green wood, moist decayed wood, damp animal dung, and similar substances.

If there is any scarcity of fuel, it may be preferable to keep only a small fire going if that is necessary for comfort and to concentrate on heaping up signal pyres to be lit at a moment's notice.

The smoke from a strong smudge fire can, incidentally, be invaluable for indicating wind direction to the pilot of a rescue plane.

Three Smokes

The distress signal most commonly used is made with three fires or three smokes. If these are built in a conspicuous location in a straight line, their intent will be the more apparent. We can also send smoke signals from a single conflagration by momentarily cutting off the smoke with something such as a wet blanket and releasing series of three puffs.

Ingenuity

When no natural fuel at all is available, a possibility for instance if we are in an aircraft forced down in a desert, some improvisation can generally be made such as, under those particular circumstances, scraping a sign for help in the sand and when a plane is nearby filling the depressions with gasoline and igniting that.

Distress Signals

The most universally recognized distress signals are based on the number three; three flashes, three shots, and so forth, even to the three dots, three dashes, three dots of the familiar SOS.

There is, unfortunately, no general agreement as to how signal shots ought to be spaced. Some advocate firing the three blasts as rapidly as possible, although obviously it is not unusual for a hunter to let drive in this fashion at game. The practice of separating each shot by about five seconds is more logical, especially as this gives an experienced listener the time he may need to determine where the signal is coming from. In any event, an understanding on this point may well be reached in advance by members of a group.

Party Signals

One of the simplest and most valuable precautions a party in a wilderness area can take is to agree upon a set of signals for its own use. These should be both brief and uncomplicated, and should take into account all reasonable contingencies such as the possibility that any member of the group may be short of ammunition. It will be well to set this code down on paper, so that each individual can carry a copy with him at all times, possibly rolled within his waterproof match case.

Whistle

A whistle can be particularly handy for signaling in remote regions. The Hudson's Bay Company includes a whistle in its survival kits with the succinct instructions: "Use your whistle to gain or keep contact with other members of your party. It may also be used to notify anyone close enough to hear of your position. Don't shout or call. Blow the whistle."

Dots and Dashes

Knowledge of a dot-and-dash code will enable the sending and receiving of messages with flashlight, mirror, whistle, smoke, radio, and numerous other devices including the primitive thumping of a hollow log.

In case you ever undertake to memorize such a code, may I suggest in the interests of saving your time that you do not make the error I did of thinking in terms of dots and dashes. When you hear a dit-dah, for example, you'll save an unnecessary mental process by recognizing that directly as "a" without having to go to the trouble of figuring that dit-dah is really dot-dash which, in turn, is the first letter in the alphabet.

Wigwagging

Such signals transmitted by flag can be seen for miles under favorable conditions, particularly if the sender places himself in an unobstructed spot against a contrasting background. Reading with the help of glasses, we have thus sent messages from mountain to mountain.

The flag may be something such as a large handkerchief or

shirt, knotted to the end of a light pole some six feet long so as to expose an easily distinguishable area. It can usually be most easily manipulated if the base of the staff is held at waist level in the palm of one hand and the stick gripped a dozen inches or so higher by the master hand.

All letters start with the staff held straight upward. The dot is made by swinging the flag down to the right and then back again. A way to fix this in mind is to remember that the word "right" has a dot over the "i." It will follow that the

The International Morse Code which is the most widely understood follows:

Flag	Letters	Intervals
right-left	A	short-long
left-right-right-right	B	long-short-short-short
left-right-left-right	C	long-short-long-short
left-right-right	D	long-short-short
right	E	short
right-right-left-right	F	short-short-long-short
left-left-right	G	long-long-short
right-right-right-right	H	short-short-short-short
right-right	I	short-short
right-left-left-left	J	short-long-long-long
left-right-left	K	long-short-long
right-left-right-right	L	short-long-short-short
left-left	M	long-long
left-right	N	long-short
left-left-left	O	long-long-long
right-left-left-right	P	short-long-long-short
left-left-right-left	Q	long-long-short-long
right-left-right	R	short-long-short
right-right-right	S	short-short-short
left	T	long
right-right-left	U	short-short-long
right-right-right-left	V	short-short-short-long
right-left-left	W	short-long-long
left-right-right-left	X	long-short-short-long
left-right-left-left	Y	long-short-long-long
left-left-right-right	Z	long-long-short-short

dash is made by swinging the flag in a similar arc to the left and back. You'll find that the easiest way to keep the flag flat, for maximum visibility, will be to move it in tight loops. To send the letter "n," swing left and back and then right and back in what is, when you look up at the tip of the staff, a narrow figure eight.

Hold the flag upright a moment to end a letter. Lower and raise it in front of you to finish a word. Swinging right-left-right-left-right will signify the conclusion of a message, although the important factor in any kind of emergency signaling is not correctness of form but common sense.

Uses for a Mirror

A mirror may certainly be included with good reason among the equipment to be carried on the person in the bush, if only for the assistance thus afforded in removing the bits of bark and other particles that always seem to be getting in the eyes. A surface of ordinary metal, such as the back of a watch, is a poor substitute in this respect. Furthermore, an adequate mirror can be vital if one ever needs to attract attention in an emergency.

The substantial Emergency Signaling Mirror available for a few cents at many surplus stores is a particularly useful article to have in a pocket. Its range under ideal conditions is limited only by the curvature of the earth, and with it in bright weather you have a good chance of attracting anyone you can see.

Even if no rescuer is visible, the practice of sweeping the horizon with an aimed beam of reflected sunlight is recommended for, as most of us can testify, the way in which even a distant tiny flash from something as small as a dewdrop can catch the eye is startling.

The Hudson's Bay Company includes such a double-faced mirror in its emergency kits, with the following advice: "If the angle of the sun and the aeroplane or surface ship is not too great (90° maximum), you can hold the mirror three to six inches from your face and sight at the plane through the small hole in the center.

If you see an aeroplane or surface ship during the day when the sun is shining, your double-faced mirror may be used for signaling.

a. If the angle of the sun and the aeroplane or surface ship is not too great (90° max.), you can hold the mirror three to six inches away from your face and sight at the plane through the small hole in the center. The light from the sun shining through the hole will form a spot of light on your face and this spot will be reflected in the rear surface of the mirror. Then, still sighting on the aeroplane through the hole, adjust the angle of the mirror until the reflection of the light spot on the rear of the mirror coincides with the hole in the mirror and disappears. The reflected light will now be accurately aimed at the plane.

FIG. 54. Signaling by mirror.

"The light from the sun shining through the hole will form a spot of light on your face, and this spot will be reflected in the rear surface of the mirror. Then, still sighting on the aeroplane through the hole, adjust the angle of the mirror until the reflection of the light spot on the rear of the mirror coincides with the hole in the mirror and disappears. The reflected light will now be accurately aimed at the plane.

"If the angle between the target and the sun is great (more than 90°), sight the aeroplane through the hole, then adjust

b. If the angle between the target and the sun is great (more than 90°), hold the mirror as shown, sight the aeroplane through the hole, then adjust the angle of the mirror until the reflection of the light spot on your hand coincides with the hole in the mirror and disappears. This method will work where the aeroplane or ship is almost on one horizon and the sun almost 180° away on the opposite horizon.

FIG. 54. Signaling by mirror (continued)

the angle of the mirror until the reflection of the light spot on your hand coincides with the hole in the mirror and disappears. This method will work where the aeroplane or ship is almost on one horizon and the sun almost 180° away on the opposite horizon."

The Hudson's Bay Company illustrations herein reproduced otherwise speak for themselves. The double-faced emergency mirror issued for the armed forces of the United States, made with a small open cross for facilitating aiming, can be employed in the same manner.

Any reflecting surface, even a flat piece of wood that is slick with moisture, can be used instead of a mirror. By punching a small hole in the center of something such as a flattened can, sufficiently shiny on both sides, you will be able to improvise a sight for aiming a reflected beam.

International Silent Periods

If you should happen to have a radio, the most likely times to send distress signals will be during the three-minute international silent periods which commence at fifteen minutes before and at fifteen minutes after each hour Greenwich time.

Body Signals

There are certain established body signals that will be recognized by most airmen.

Do you require urgent medical assistance? Then as you probably already know, lie on your back with arms stretched straight behind you. Another widely used signal indicating severe injury is the crossing of the arms across the body.

Standing erect with the left arm hanging at the side and the right arm upraised signifies: "Everything is all right. Do not wait."

If still leaving the left hand at the side you hold the right arm horizontal, that means you will be able to proceed shortly and that the plane should wait if practical.

If you continue to stand erect and lift both arms horizontal, you need either mechanical help or parts, and there will be a long delay on your part.

Standing and holding both arms straight above your head means that you want to be picked up.

Swinging your hands sidewise back and forth above your head means that the observing plane should not attempt to land where you are.

If you want to signal the pilot where to come down, squat on your heels and point in the direction of the recommended landing place.

Perhaps you have a radio. If so and the receiver is working, this you can signify by cupping your hands conspicuously over your ears.

If instead you want the pilot to drop a message, swing the right hand down in front of you to shoulder height several times.

To signal in the affirmative, wave something such as a shirt or handkerchief up and down in front of you.

To signal in the negative, wave such an article back and forth in front of you.

Although signs vary with different groups, the plane can make an affirmative by dipping up and down the way the head is nodded. It can show negation by a slight zigzag motion comparable to shaking the head. Green flashes from a signaling lamp or the aircraft's rocking from side to side is an acknowledgment that the plane has understood the message;

red flashes on the signaling lamp or a complete right hand circuit that it hasn't.

Symbols

Symbols designed to be seen and interpreted from the air can be fashioned with boughs, stones, and lengths of various materials such as strips of cloth. They can be formed by such methods as digging or scratching lines, and by trudging back and forth in snow until trenches that will loom up black to a plane are made; these impressions being extended north and south whenever possible so as to be most conspicuous in sunlight strong enough to cast a shadow. Another way to capitalize on constrasting darkness in snowy terrain is to floor such trenches with evergreen boughs and to heap shadow-throwing snow on the southern sides of the symbols.

Any such symbols will naturally be put down in as prominent and conspicuous a location as is available. You'll make them large, perhaps an easily visible ten feet thick and, depending on locality and expediency, possibly one hundred feet or more long. Color contrast can be vital.

An arrow with the point heading the way you intend to go will indicate you are proceeding in a particular direction. Perhaps you'll want the plane to show you which way to go. Then put out a large "K." The pilot will probably take note of it by waggling the wings, after which he'll head in the correct direction for a significant period of time.

A long straight line means you need urgent medical assistance. Two long straight lines denote that although a doctor is not required, you do want medical supplies. A cross is the sign that you are unable to proceed by yourself, perhaps because of serious injury. A triangle: "Probably safe to land here."

You can indicate negation with a big "N." Yes is "Y." "L L" means that all is well. Are you hungry and perhaps thirsty? Then make a big "F." A square will show that you would like a map and compass. Two V's, one inside the other, is the request for firearms and ammunition.

Coast Guard Signals

Certain distress signals are used by the U. S. Coast Guard. A red light, red rocket, or flare at night indicates that you have been seen and that assistance will be forthcoming as soon as possible.

Haul away is signaled by waving a red flag from shore during daylight and by displaying at night a red light, red rocket, or red roman candle.

Slack away is indicated when a white flag is waved from the shore by day. Waving a white light slowly back and forth, firing a white rocket, or setting off a white roman candle means the same thing by night.

Waving a white flag and a red flag at the same time from the shore during daylight is a signal that landing in your own boat is impossible. Slowly waving a white light and red light at the same time means the same thing. So does a blue light at night.

The beckoning during daylight by a man ashore or the burning of two torches close together at night indicates that particular spot is the best place to land.

Any of these signals can be answered by the craft or individual to which they are directed by the waving of a flag, a shirt, a hand, or anything else that can be seen by daylight. Response at night may be by rocket, gun, blue light, or by briefly showing a light over the ship's gunwale and then hiding it.

A Simple Way to Prevent Tragedy

An extremely simple precaution that would save thousands of hours of needless effort, anxiety, and agony every season is for each of us to make his plans known every time we are about to head into the bush. If no responsible individual is present to whom to entrust this information, we can do worse than to note it briefly in a dated message and to leave that in some safe and prominent place.

Even when we park an automobile beside the highway with the idea of perhaps fishing for an hour, it would take us only a moment or two to jot down that information and to wedge the paper, in a sealed envelope if desired, securely beneath a windshield wiper. No one would be apt to disturb it unless we failed to return for a disproportionate length of time, and any one of us can think of numerous reasons why we might somehow be delayed and in need of help.

Chapter 20

Getting Out By Yourself

ANYONE WHO merely happens to stray from his way is seldom faced with much of an external problem although internal conflicts may become considerable, for the brain of man can impose very alarming obstacles where none have been placed by nature.

These mental and therefore all the more unnerving obstructions are under such circumstances most often the immediate results of either panic or pride, the first of which will sometimes set the ordinarily most rational of men running crazily, while the second can at the least spur him to continue blundering aimlessly after dark when there may be real danger of injury.

Finding Yourself

To stay lost in comparatively well settled country one would really, although perhaps subconsciously, have to work at it. Hiking in a straight line in any direction would bring him out, and this he could do even without a compass by continuing to line up two objects ahead of him. These might be two trees. When he had almost reached the nearer of these, he would select another sight in line further ahead.

Sound will often lead one toward habitation. So will smoke.

A bare knoll or safely climbed tree may reveal a house. Walls and fences generally lead somewhere, and although this may be only to a long deserted farm, the deep ruts of some ancient path will then in all likelihood wind toward a more recently traveled way.

Suppose It's Not Your Road

Although such a precaution would seem so elemental as not to merit mentioning, if one is really lost no road should be spurned just because it may not seem to be the right road.

Yet even in Alaska Highway country—a wilderness as large as all Europe west of prewar Russia and normally inhabited until recently by scarcely enough people to fill the Rose Bowl—trackers have seen where lost men trying to find their way have crossed this engineering epic two and three times. On each occasion they've deliberately left the wilderness road to blunder back into the bush, where they could easily travel in a straight line for as many weeks and months as they could keep going before coming across another manmade thoroughfare of any description.

Common Sense

When someone is lost, if there is one essential any more important than another it is common sense, this to be exercised not only by the individual in difficulty but by his companions as well. It was when I was hunting with Charles Ballou over one of his New Hampshire cuttings that this New England lumberman mentioned the illustrative episode.

A sportsman was late one evening in making his way out of a rough patch of woodland about one mile square. His friends started driving around and around the road that bounded the area, blowing the horn more and more frantically every few minutes. The hunter started out in one direction, corrected his line, changed it again, began hastening still another way, and finally become so exhausted and confused that he was not able to get out until daylight.

Agree on Definite Procedure

Any group functioning in the farther places will do well to agree beforehand on definite procedure to be used in any apparent emergency. Unless the individuals have been going together into the bush for a long time, they may choose to commit this plan to paper so that each can carry a copy. Sensible courses of action will depend largely upon terrain, climate, circumstances, and upon the experience and capabilities of those involved.

Walking Out

Opinions naturally differ at least as often as do the viewpoints from which they are formed, but few will disagree that if we may have to cover a considerable distance, the pace to take is one we will be able to follow all day and still have a reserve of energy left over. We will be apt to end up wasting time if we attempt to press.

Most of us find, too, that we can maintain better and therefore safer balance by keeping the feet pointed as nearly straight ahead as is comfortable, and that we are often able to pick up an additional inch or two per step this way, while coming up on the toes will so use these members as to afford both extra distance and impetus.

It usually requires a disproportionate amount of energy to travel straight up and down hills, as the trails of animals reveal they well know. We will generally do better in the long run either to zigzag or to slant off at a gradual pitch. Energy will be conserved if you can proceed without cutting across major drainage systems. As for resting, this is more beneficial when enjoyed frequently for brief periods. Hurrying ahead for long stretches and then taking prolonged breathing spells tends, as one discovers early in life, to cause the muscles to stiffen.

Anyone making a forced hike will do well to change sox about the middle of the day if this is possible. The feet will probably be the most vulnerable part of the body in such an eventuality and should, only logically, be attended to in ratio to their importance. The best ordinary procedure is to carry a number of small adhesive bandages whenever in the bush and to apply one of these without delay whenever any irritation is felt.

A sensible formula finally to repeat to ourselves and therefore to heed whenever covering ground afoot in the wilderness, I believe you will concur upon analyzing it, is: Never step on anything you can step over, and never step over anything you can step around.

If You'd Rather Raft

Because rivers are the great highways of many vast wilderness stretches, it may be the knowledge of how to build and use a raft that will bring you through hundreds of miles of primitive regions to safety.

If you ever have to construct such a raft and have had no previous experience in such matters, you may be interested to know that the reason three long logs can be used so satisfactorily for such a job is that a conveyance built on such a nucleus can be either readily paddled or poled, depending on the water. Drifting, it can be steered with a long oar, sweep, or some other rudder arrangement. A short square raft, on the other hand, has too much tendency to spin.

The raft should be made if possible of sound dry wood, perhaps from dead trees that are still standing. In the absence of spikes, the three logs can be lashed together with roots, vines, small limber withes, or fibrous bark. With an ax, however, you can do a really professional job. A knife can be em-

FIG. 55. Notching log for raft.

ployed instead although laboriously. In the absence of such tools, you might burn out the necessary openings.

The work may be commenced by laying the three logs in

position near the water. You are going to need two substantial crosspieces across the top, one near each end. A couple of tough, rugged poles will do. Set these in place and mark on the logs beneath where each pole is to go.

Then cut the six notches so that each is narrow at the top, widening as it goes deeper into the log. When the two crosspieces are finally driven through each series of three notches, the fit should be snug. Once the raft has been allowed to soak, it will then become even more firmly interlocked.

Some Rules of Rafting

You will be only prudent if you take every possible precaution when using such a raft, particularly under the stress and uncertainty of emergency conditions. Keep listening and watching as far ahead as possible, for some notable patches of bad water such as the colloquially named Parlez Pos Rapids of the Peace River give no warning until one is almost in them. For this reason, it is a sound idea to scout ahead whenever this is at all feasible.

If you have a rope, you may be able to line the raft through rapids while walking safely along or near shore. Otherwise, you will probably do better to let the raft go with the idea of retrieving it later if that is possible.

You will have to provide as well as you can for the safety of any outfit you may have along, perhaps in one of two ways:

(1) either by tying it securely to the raft, or

(2) by packing it in as waterproof a bundle as you can manage with some provision, such as the inclusion of a chunk of light dry wood, so that it will float.

Make Your Own Automatic Pilot

One day you may find yourself floating alone on such a raft down a broad sluggish river like many in the Far North. A rock, pail, or old coal oil container hung beneath the conveyance by a short line affixed to the front center of the latter will automatically tend to keep your carrier in a main channel. Besides thus acting as a guide, this arrangement can also conserve energy otherwise expended on dreary hours of steering.

Finding an Outlet

An old sourdough stunt used to locate the outlet of a quiet body of water is to float bannock crumbs or bits of some other light substances and to observe which way they drift.

Advantages of Winter Travel

Although the winter of fiction closes the northern wildernesses, the winter of reality opens much such country, freezing streams providing highways that twine enticingly through regions otherwise difficult to penetrate. Along the edges of rivers, a smooth icy sidewalk is often repaved week after week by congealing overflow.

For those on snowshoes, the deepening whiteness becomes a level carpet over jackpots of brush and tangled deadfall. Because of both ice and snow, therefore, one is often able to save hours and even days of travel by proceeding in straight lines that otherwise would be impossible on foot.

Better Visibility and Audibility

There are other reasons why anyone who finds himself stranded in the blanched wilderness of North America in winter will in some respects have a better chance of getting out than he would during any other season. Two of these reasons arise from the fact that the colder it becames, the farther it is possible to see and to hear. Either phenomenon may be of the utmost value to anyone stranded or lost.

When temperatures fall eighty and ninety degrees below freezing on the Peace River, the ring of axes at Hudson Hope five miles downstream resounds distinctly at our homesite. On still days when the temperature is close to the melting point, I haven't been able to hear Dudley Shaw, our nearest neighbor, working diligently at from one-half to one-third of that distance away.

It is often difficult, especially when one is a stranger to primitive regions, to determine from what direction a sound is coming. This ability we can develop with practice, but in the meantime one way to get a bearing when the noise is prolonged enough is to turn the head until it seems loudest. Holding a hand over one ear may make this more perceptible. Closing the eyes also reduces distractions for some individuals. If you have an opportunity, of course, you'll stand in an open place as far as possible from any broad reflecting surfaces such as cliffs.

How to Make Emergency Snowshoes

You will do the best you can, and in a pinch this action may hinge on the fact that one can often get along much better than otherwise by the very simple expediency of attaching broad light evergreen boughs to the feet.

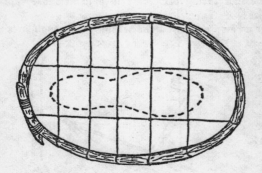

FIG. 56. Emergency snowshoes.

You may be able to travel without even these aids by sticking to where snow lies thinnest; along the edges of streams scoured by wind, atop northern rims and benches where the melting sun has made its influence felt, and in heavy evergreen groves where storms have not fallen so deeply. Warm dry chinook winds, which some Indians call snow-eaters, are so pleasantly prevalent in many northern areas that there one seldom has to take to webs.

If you ever do have to improvise snowshoes, you will have a rough idea of how to proceed if only from pictures that you have seen. Where obstructions are not too thick, the circular bear-paw type will be the simplest to build and use. A narrower and longer shoe will be essential if you have to follow a tighter trail.

Frames can be made by bending live wood into the shape desired, green saplings being thawed first, of course, in sunlight or near a fire if the sap is frozen.

Strips of rawhide will make satisfactory emergency webbing. Animals on the party are sometimes killed to furnish this, as when a pack outfit is trapped in the mountains by early autumn blizzards. You can use the green strips. These should be heavier where the foot is directly supported. In slick going, portions of hide attached beneath the snowshoes with the hair facing back may help to decrease slipping on upgrades.

Rope is also employed for webbing, although it is a nuis-

FIG. 57. An improvised bow drill may be used for drilling snowshoe frames. The point may be made from a nail or wire.

ance in frigid going because of the manner in which it continues to stretch as cold deepens. It may have to be loosened in slushy travel, on the other hand, lest it pull and break the frames. Rawhide also happens to be an annoyance under these latter conditions, sagging and stretching as it does when wet.

One pair of emergency webs that got their wearer out of the bush near our cabin was strung with snare wire, around each strand of which moosehide strips had been twisted.

The size of any emergency snowshoes will be governed by conditions. They will be preferably as small and as light as will support one on the snow over which he has to travel. If this forest covering is deep and soft, the shoes may have to be six feet long and one foot wide. The webbing, too, should then be closer together.

Reaching Safety

Many northern trappers prefer to attach webs to their feet with a simple harness made of some fabric, lamp wicking being a favorite. You may also use a single broad strap, lacing it to the snowshoe so as to provide a loop into which the instep can be thrust. In any event, you will want the front of the snowshoe to swing up out of the way by its own weight when the foot is lifted.

There is no intricate technique to snowshoeing. Just put them on and start walking. Various improvisations will suggest themselves according to the particular circumstances. When the going becomes tough, some oldtimers help themselves along simply by knotting a line to the tip of each snowshoe so that they can assist by hand the swinging of the web up and ahead each step; sustaining the assertion that half the confusion of the world comes from not realizing how little we need.

PART FOUR

SAFETY

"Survival is merely a question of knowing where the dangers are and how to recognize them, and how to take advantage of the resources offered by the country."

—*Royal Canadian Mounted Police*

Chapter 21

Keeping Out Of Trouble

ONCE ONE realizes though only subconsciously that circumstances are such that he can not afford to have an accident, probabilities shift markedly against any mishap befalling him, and nowhere is this more apparent than under the drastic law of the wild. For what may be but a self-punishing, or attention-getting, or a responsibility-relieving misstep where help is at hand, can be fatal when one is alone.

The only reasonable rule in remote regions anywhere is not to take unnecessary chances, weighing always the possible loss against the potential gain, and going about life with as wide a safety margin as practical.

"Nothing is so much to be feared as fear," Thoreau noted, but he added, "A live dog is preferable to a dead lion."

Center of Gravity

When we are descending a cut bank or in fact any downgrade, a basic safety principle—which we all recognize but sometimes overlook in the exhilaration of a descent—is so to control our center of gravity that if we do fall, it will be backwards in maneuverable sliding position.

Such a precaution, we come more and more to realize, is of the utmost importance during solitary travel over new paths, where loose shale has not before been by man disturbed and where decomposing logs have not been tried.

The identical principle holds even when we are traveling among obstructions on a flat, for it is a sometimes too costly convenience to let the body drop or swing forward so as to rest a hand momentarily on a projection and vault ahead. The untested support to which we will then be committed may roll, slide, or give away entirely. Even though this may happen only one time in ten thousand in such a way that we will still not be able to save ourselves, unless there are extenuating circumstances the odds will still be too far out of proportion to warrant the taking of such a gamble.

Figure to Fall

A reasonably precautionary attitude back of beyond is to expect to fall at any moment, for so realizing the possibility, we will be more likely to be prepared for it:

(1) by avoidance of an area,

(2) by extreme care when to bypass is not practical,

(3) and most commonly by continually gauging beforehand where and in what manner, if we do fall, we will be able to let ourselves go most safely.

Deadfalls project an especial hazard, and one that is greatly multiplied when the ground is at all wet. Dew can make a fallen log so slippery that the feet will fly out from beneath one so unexpectedly that any control is at once gone. Frost imposes graver danger. Especially tricky is dead bark that all of a sudden turns on the trunk itself.

It would be pointless to indicate that all such perils may be avoided by keeping off of fallen timber, for we often find that a down tree is by far the most reasonable way over a ravine or flooded creek. We occasionally come upon vast stretches of old burn where the only way across is atop a maze of deadfall. What we may logically choose to do, therefore, is to test such footings as carefully as possible and to proceed with maximum caution, taking secure hand holds whenever they are offered, while limiting and when possible excluding any tightrope walking and leaping.

Fording

By studying the character of a stream we can often most closely gauge how best to cross it, for except in still water the most shallow part is generally where the current is widest.

It is not necessary to explain why a stout pole is useful during actual wading, for most of us are as reluctant as anyone else to implant our feet blindly when it is possible to test the footing ahead, while even less effective means of steadying ourselves against a tugging torrent are not to be disregarded lightly. Any packs, of course, we will hold loosely enough to be swiftly disengaged if necessary.

Despite any natural reluctance to get wet unnecessarily, no one will disagree but that it is often better to wet the feet deliberately than to attempt a hazardous passage across slippery logs or uncertain stepping stones.

If there is much of a flow to be crossed, we may decide that the most comfortable procedure will be to remove clothing with the idea of keeping it dry until it can be again donned. Because we will want to afford our feet the utmost protection, however, we will on occasion deem it advisable to replace boots or shoes for the fording. When wiped out and put back on, either over dry hose or over damp woolen stockings that have been squeezed as free of water as possible, most footgear suitable for the wilderness will be no more than momentarily uncomfortable.

Waves

In connection with water, there is one especial precaution that anyone venturing along a rocky open seacoast should heed. That is to hold fast at the first feasible spot upon the approach of a big wave, deliberately choosing a wetting rather than taking the chance of running across uncertain footing and thus risking, in many exposed areas, the very real peril of being injured and even of being swept away and drowned.

Visibility

Visibility is sometimes so deceptively restricted in dangerous terrain that it is foolhardy to keep going, if to continue is necessary, without taking special precautions. A low hanging cloud, sudden sleet, and the way snow and dust occasionally smoke up in stinging particles before an eye-watering wind can make travel almost blind.

Depending on where we are, we may break off evergreen tips and keep one or two thrown always well ahead of us to mark an apparently safe passage. This procedure we may well augment by cutting a long dry stick, light enough to wield easily, and by poking about on all sides to minimize the possibility of stepping off into undetected emptiness.

How to Make a Torch

"The temptation to stay in good country as long as light lasts is inevitable," as Colonel Townsend Whelen notes. "In the Northeast woods were white birch trees are plentiful, a birchbark torch has often brought me safe and sound to camp.

"Strip a piece of birchbark a foot wide and about three feet long from the tree. Fold this in three folds lengthwise, making a three-fold strip about four inches by three feet. Split one end of a three-foot pole for carrying, the split of the pole engaging the bark strip about eight inches from one end and keeping it from unfolding. Light the short eight-inch end.

"If you want more light turn the lighted end downward so the fire will burn up on the bark. If it burns too fast, turn the burning end upward. As the bark is consumed, pull more of it through the split in the stick handle. Such a strip will last fifteen to twenty minutes and will light all the ground, trees, and bushes within about twenty feet. When the bark is about half consumed, look for another tree from which to get more bark."

Exhaustion

When one is excited by the challenge of covering ground, exhaustion often creeps on unrecognized. This can be so much more serious a problem in severe weather that particularly when it is cold and stormy, one will generally be well advised in strange country under survival conditions to pick a camping spot early enough to be able to prepare for as comfortable a night as possible.

For what interest it may hold, here is the way some of our trapper friends gauge their strength. The trapper reaches one of the cabins on his line. He is not conscious of feeling particularly tired. Can he proceed to the next cabin? He stands and looks up at the heavens. If the sky seems to keep receding before his eyes, he takes that as a sure sign he is too near the limit of his strength to risk going farther. So he turns in where he is.

Sharp Tools

The general precaution you may observe when using knife and ax is to expect the cutting edge to slip or drive untrue, and so to handle them that if this does happen no injury will result.

We can also get into all sorts of unexpected trouble when carrying sharp tools of this type, and the following two examples may serve to indicate the lengths which precautions may well extend. One sourdough thrust his bare ax, blade downward, under the lashings at the side of his dog sled. When the dogs started running at the sight of a moose, he overturned the sled and flung himself across it as he had on other occasions to anchor the team. This time he suffered a bad gash. Another old-timer drove his ax into a section of firewood which he shouldered having finished that work for the day. When he dropped the chunk off by his cabin, an exposed corner of the blade slashed his leg.

It is therefore no more prudent than anyone of us might expect to keep points and edges of such tools strapped whenever feasible within sufficiently heavy sheaths that are adequately secured as by copper rivets.

Knots

Knowing how to tie a few very simple knots will not only serve on occasion to keep difficulties from developing, but it is not at all improbable if one spends much time in farther places that such knowledge may one day be vital.

Knots vary a little in design, depending on their uses, but the principles remain the same, as any not knowing so already can see by the accompanying illustrations. What we want in the majority of instances is a knot that will not let go but which, at the same time, can be untied in a hurry.

Basically important is the square knot that when improperly tied becomes the disreputable granny knot which commits the double fault of jamming and slipping. The slightly different sheet bend is effective for joining two ropes of different sizes.

One is always finding uses for the very simple two half-hitches. The clove hitch, which is merely a pair of half-

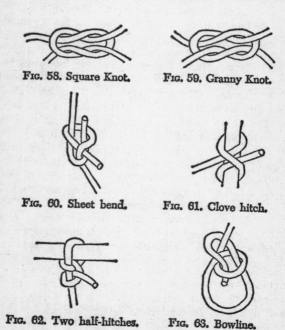

FIG. 58. Square Knot.   FIG. 59. Granny Knot.

FIG. 60. Sheet bend.   FIG. 61. Clove hitch.

FIG. 62. Two half-hitches.   FIG. 63. Bowline.

hitches made in opposite directions, is handy for fastening a rope to a tree trunk.

The quickly tied and untied bowline, which has raised and lowered tens of thousands of individuals to safety, provides a loop that will neither tighten nor slip.

A practical way to tie the same type of knot by feel alone if, as we often do, you want to picket a horse by a foreleg at night, is first to make a loop near the end of a rope and then to pull the standing part of the rope through it in a second loop as shown by the drawing. Hold this second loop in one hand and the rope end in the other. Pass the short end not too snugly below the fetlock just above the hoof, shove the end into the second loop, and by pulling the second loop back through the first work the knot into position. See Page 228.

Ice Never Safe

Ice travel can never be considered safe, inasmuch as even when temperatures drop one hundred degrees below freezing, some parts of northern rivers not only always remain open, but other portions are sheathed with ice so thin it will scarcely support its own weight. Overflow creates other hazardous conditions. So does the dropping of water levels, leaving great sheets of ice suspended. As for cracks of various widths and depths, they are ever characteristic.

Other dangers build up when an insulating rug of snow shields ice from the hardening effects of cold, while running water beneath is eroding it. When ice is bare, its quality of magnification—which makes possible the use of a lens of ice to start a campfire—can under the glare of sunlight create temperatures dangerously above thawing.

Safety cannot always consist in keeping off ice, for if we are making our way through a northern wilderness in winter, particularly under emergency conditions, ice travel may very likely open the most practical routes. The solution must lie instead in taking all reasonable safety precautions while on ice.

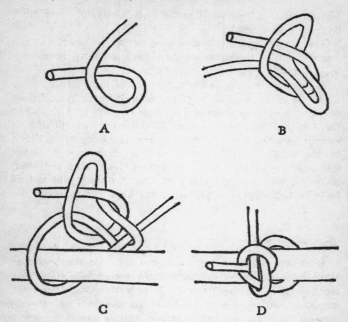

Fig. 64. How to tie nonslipping and nonjamming knot by feel alone.

Carrying a Pole

An elementary safeguard to take whenever you can during ice travel is to carry horizontally a long light pole which, if you plunge unexpectedly below the general level as is possible anywhere at any moment, can serve automatically as a bridge both to check the descent and to afford a ready means of extrication.

The practice of bearing a slender length of dry wood becomes less a nuisance than second nature, particularly as with it you can conveniently jab at suspicious portions ahead such as those hidden beneath snow or under a frozen skim of overflow. If with a companion, you may want instead or in addition to travel some twenty feet or so apart in single file with a rope between you.

Reading Streams

We can read the character of a strange stream to a certain extent from the formation of its banks and thus keep whenever reasonable to shallows. Sheer banks are apt to continue their steepness beneath water, as we all know, making for comparatively deep conditions nearby. A gradual bank, on the other hand, presupposes the likelihood of shoals, although there are numerous exceptions which vary for the most part according to local geology.

Candle Ice and Seasonal Dangers

When the congealed moisture of winter begins musically to seek the sea or to migrate to other climes in clouds, ice along the shore thaws, making the immediate problem one of reaching the still solid masses farther out. The procedure usually is to follow the shore until a jam or some other approach, such as a series of rocks, is located.

Dangers of ice travel multiply rapidly at this time of the year when the sinking swish of snow enlivens the land, and not the least of the hazards then arising is that imposed by candle ice.

Ice will still seem solid to the inexperienced eye when, as a matter of fact, it has disintegrated to candle ice so treacherous that anyone not knowing better may step on an apparently stable area and sink through it as if it were slush. The unexpectedness with which this can happen may be better appreciated when we realize that ice several feet thick often decomposes into long vertical needles, and that among these the testing pole can be driven all the way through in a single jab.

Candle ice, which has caused the drownings of numerous sourdoughs and natives, is best shunned entirely, particularly because of the difficulty of regaining safety after one has got into trouble.

Wolves

The wolf is so cautious that, aided by a high order of intelligence, it will put forth every effort not to be even seen by man. Its correspondingly keen curiosity, however, will sometimes lead to close investigations especially during protective darkness, and this has stimulated some of the tales about wolves trailing individuals with the alleged motive of eventually attacking.

Whenever I hear such accounts I think of many nights in the Continental Northwest when I've gone to sleep wherever in the wilderness I have happened to be, many times listening as I dozed off to a wolf chorus and often as not hearing the wild music when half-awakening during the night but—except for the thrill it still never ceases to arouse—having no particular emotion except the pleasure of feeling more closely attuned to the unspoiled places; not because of any daring but because I soon realized, both from observation and from what others told me, that no wolf will harm a human being.

Men Make Animals React Dangerously

Wild animals who have been handled enough by men to lose their natural fear of human beings, as for example a fawn brought up on a bottle, may occasionally become dangerous.

Males of the deer family as a whole sometimes prove truculent during rutting seasons, while later a mother may try to send an intruder away if she thinks her young are threatened. So, for example, will a bear. So will a tiny swallow. And if someone then runs, apparently frightened, the often followed impulse of both bear and swallow is to chase.

Sometimes, too, an animal will flee at a sound or odor and, not seeing an individual, may appear to be charging him. An animal who is or believes himself cornered may try to wipe a man out of the way. As for wounded animals, even a tiny squirrel will bite and scratch.

Suppose you come face to face with a large animal that shows no disposition to sift into the shadows? The best thing to do is to stand perfectly still and, my experience has been although all may not agree, to talk in as calm and as even a manner as possible. The choice of words makes no difference, for any unexcited and not unfriendly human monotone appears to have a soothing effect on an animal. Any I have so met in the open have, unless they bolted immediately, regarded me for a brief time and then moved away, usually slowly and in any event without sign of overmuch excitement.

If you have a firearm, you will naturally get that in position as calmly and as smoothly as possible, particularly if the animal is at such close quarters that any abruptness may provoke a similar reaction. Any movement should therefore be so extremely gradual as to be almost imperceptible. Unless absolutely necessary, it will seldom be wise under such conditions to shoot.

Suppose the animal shows no indication that it will give ground? You may prefer to leave with as much of an appearance of casualness as you can manifest, continuing to avoid any sudden movements and still talking quietly.

Greater Living Hazards Than Beasts

Insects are considerably more dangerous in the wilderness than any wild animals, and in fact mosquitoes and black flies become so thick in many regions of the United States and Canada that they can actually kill a full grown man in good health who is lost or stranded without sufficient knowledge or ingenuity to protect himself.

Modern insect repellents can solve the problem more quickly and easily than anything else, short of keeping inside an enclosure whose openings are protected with fine netting. Present compounds are colorless, do not damage most clothing, and have an odor not at all disagreeable to most individuals, whereas the old pine tar products used to dirty everything and were not particularly effective to boot. These newer repellents are being so continually improved that it will be well to check with several as informed sources as you can contact as to what at the moment is best for your purpose.

Smoke, too, will help discourage the pests while one is camped. Mud plastered on exposed parts will afford protection during travel. Plugging the ears lightly with cotton will often make buzzing insects a lot more bearable. Inadequate clothing can be reinforced with some wild substance, a sheath of birchbark beneath the stockings for example adding protection for the legs. The most comfortable provision is to keep whenever possible to windy stretches such as bare ridges and wide shores.

Chapter 22

Getting Out Of Trouble

"A MAN sits as many risks as he runs," Thoreau pointed out. "The amount of it is, if a man is alive, there is always danger that he may die."

Upon Falling Through Ice

One tool to have within easy reach during ice travel is a sheath knife, particularly when other safeguards such as a pole are lacking, and on particularly dangerous stretches you, too, may want to hold this ready in a hand. Then if you do go through, you'll have the immediate chance to drive the point into solid ice and with its aid to roll yourself out and away from danger.

Another method in cold weather of then obtaining traction is, as quick as thought, to reach out to the fullest extent of your arms and to bring down your wet sleeves and gloves against firm ice where, if temperatures are low enough, they will almost instantly freeze.

If weather conditions are more temperate, you may have to break away thin ice with your hands so as to reach a surface strong enough to hold your full weight. It is usually possible in the meantime to support yourself by resting a hand or arm flatly on fragile ice. Then if there seems to be no better way, get as much of your arms as you can over the edge, bring your body as nearly horizontal as is possible with the help perhaps of a swimming motion with the feet, and get a leg over and roll toward safety.

Snow as a Blotter

Upon breaking through ice into water and quickly scrambling out again, as occurs not infrequently during travel in the whitened wilderness, it is usually advantageous to roll at once in preferably soft and fluffy snow. If the outer clothing is somewhat water repellent, the snow will blot up much of the moisture before it can reach the body.

Any remaining dampness will in very cold weather freeze almost immediately. One advantage of this will be that the resulting sheath of ice will act as a windbreak.

Among the disadvantages will be the weight thus added. Another will be that this ice, depending on its thickness, can turn the garments into something not too gently resembling armor. Most hazardous will be the clothing's losing part or most of its ability to keep the body warm.

If a boot becomes immersed in overflow as is a common occurrence, often you can—as Dudley Shaw showed me my first week in Peace River country—step into a snowbank quickly enough that sufficient water will be absorbed to prevent any from penetrating to the foot. Sourdoughs, I learned from my friend who is among the more famous of them, occasionally so treat their footgear deliberately.

What to do After Sub-Zero Drenching

We usually proceed on ice as we do when traveling anywhere in the wilderness; with the assumption, in other words, that ice may give away beneath us any moment. The result is that if we do get wet, this does not usually extend beyond the outer clothing except perhaps where moisture may run down into the footwear.

We then change at least our stockings if we can. Otherwise,

we squeeze these as dry as possible, pour and wipe away perhaps with dry moss any water that is inside the boots, warm the feet if necessary against some other portion of the body such as the thighs, dress, and continue as normally.

Suppose the more unusual happens and we become thoroughly drenched? We roll as quickly as we can in the most absorbent snow close at hand, but let us suppose that not even this action is sufficient. If extra clothing is available and if the weather isn't too cold, we may be able to get the wet garments off before they freeze. Some of them, particularly if a companion is there to help, we can squeeze reasonably dry and put back on. If alone in extreme cold, however, it will be safer first to build a fire if that is feasible.

If we are going to build a fire, this should be attended to immediately, before hands become too numb. With a campfire blazing and with plenty of fuel at hand, it follows that no matter what we decide next to do we can take our time. We may want to dry out thoroughly, in which case the quickest and most comfortable way to go about it may be with the clothes on. Or we may prefer to rig a windbreak, employing the drying garments themselves.

I've done it both ways, but the most agreeable such occasion was when I happened to have a light eiderdown in my pack ashore. Viewed in retrospect, few days seem more enjoyable than those two I divided between replenishing the woodpile and reading an old Dumas novel which I'd discovered in a prospector's deserted cabin—where its pages had been tested by packrats who'd found them wanting, although I did not.

It is a slow and prolonged job for one alone to dry an outfit by an open campfire when temperatures are much below zero, particularly as the new danger to beware of is that of damaging necessary gear by attempting to complete the chore too rapidly.

What to do in Severe Weather

One will ordinarily be well advised during extremely severe weather to get into a shelter of sorts and to lay up beside a fire. If one has blankets or a warm sleeping bag, it will often be prudent under such conditions to bivouac even if means of easily making a blaze are lacking.

Individuals halted by storm or other troubles when traveling by motor vehicle often have enough coverings at hand to keep them safe until help arrives. Too many add needlessly and sometimes finally to their difficulties by running motors so as to heat unventilated cabs, thus risking carbon monoxide poisoning. Others, prompted by some inconsequential fear such as that of starvation, leave in entirely inadequate clothing what sanctuary they have and stake everything against unreasonable odds in an attempt to walk they're not sure where.

Freezing

We need to pay constant attention to all parts of the body to prevent freezing during intensely cold weather, examining exposed areas in particular to make sure they have not become stiff or devoid of feeling. Unprotected portions of the head, especially the ears, are particularly vulnerable.

If the hands are kept warm, by shoving them inside the clothing against the flesh whenever necessary, such a frostbitten part can be thawed by holding the palm against it for a few seconds. If this is attended to promptly, frost nip need be no more serious than chapped skin.

If we were to ask almost anyone what is the most common cause of accidental death in the North, the reply we'd most often get would be freezing. As a matter of fact, the correct answer is fire.

Frozen Feet

Every possible care should be taken not to freeze the feet, for although these are susceptible because of poorer circulation and because of cold's reaching them by conduction and thus speeding condensation, once this vulnerability is recognized it can be so offset that there seldom will be any good reason for such a predicament.

How should you act if a foot is actually frozen? First of all, do not delay. If you can build a fire at once, do that. Then you can very possibly thaw the foot in the heat of the blaze. Better still, you may be able to keep yourself comfortable while thawing the foot against some part of your own body such as the bare thigh. Or you may be able to warm it sufficently by contact with the abdomen of a human companion; or with an animal, if necessary one perhaps freshly killed and opened for that purpose.

What Not to Do

Anyone not sure of the best procedure in any emergency will probably do better to let common sense be his determinant rather than to follow blindly some unreasonable procedure about which he may have heard.

When we lack the personal experience that would enable us to make our own evaluation of a subject, it is natural for us to accept the opinions of others, and the unfortunate thing about this is that many widely popular beliefs are definite and positive in reverse ratio to their lack of foundation in fact. When long accepted but nevertheless wholly false tenets increase in assurance the oftener they are repeated, many times in highly regarded source material, they can not help but become the more dangerous.

Before anyone reading this rubs snow on a frostbitten ear, it is to be hoped that he will ask himself how the application of one frozen thing to another can help but be a good way to extend the freezing.

The way to lift the temperature of an area to above freezing is, reasonably enough, to apply warmth. To thaw an ear, for example, we cup it with a warm palm.

We soon learn not to rub, certainly. Chafing a frozen ear with snow in very cold weather is, we find, comparable to scrubbing a warm ear with sand and gravel. As for heating frozen flesh by friction sufficiently to thaw it, this is not only a slow process, but it can cause additional injury by tearing the sensitivized skin.

The pain that particularly indoors follows severe freezing

may be relieved, however, by holding snow or ice against the part, for heat at this stage increases the discomfort. One should not carry this relief so far, of course, as to risk refreezing.

Some disastrous results have followed the attempts, incredible as they may seem, of trying to thaw parts of the body with alcohol, gasoline, oil, salt water, and other liquids whose temperatures have been below 32° Farenheit. The erroneous theory has been that because these were not frozen, they were just the things to use to thaw something else. All one has to do is to glance at the ordinary thermometer on a subzero day to be reminded that although alcohol may not be frozen, it can still be cold enough to be expected to solidify in a very brief time a foot immersed in it.

Fast or Slow

If part of the body is seriously frozen, should it be thawed gradually or as quickly as possible? Medical doctors disagree on this, although at this writing opinion is shifting more and more towards speed.

Those favoring rapid thawing, as by soaking a foot in water as hot as ordinarily could be borne comfortably, believe that danger from gangrene becomes more of a possibility the longer the circulation is shut off. They also are of the opinion that the greater the length of time a part of the body is allowed to remain gravely frozen, the deeper the freezing may extend.

Those authorities favoring gradual thawing, by heat not much if any greater than normal body temperature, opine that there is less hazard of permanent damage to severely frozen tissues if only moderate heat is applied gently. This is the only treatment necessary, of course, in mild cases.

Should You Keep Moving in Cold Weather?

A dangerous fallacy, practically as widespread as the mistaken idea that frostbite should be thawed by rubbing snow on the affected area, is the long perpetuated theory that we should keep moving in cold weather lest we freeze. This universal although mistaken belief is often expressed more specifically. Don't fall asleep outdoors in very cold weather, you too have probably been warned, or you'll never wake up.

The opposite is true, for why should we waste strength in moving aimlessly about when that energy can be better rationed to keep us warm? Why should we risk excessive perspiration that, freezing, will only make us colder and very possibly dangerously so.

The best thing to do when caught out unexpectedly on a subzero night, it will be generally conceded, is to hole up in safe cover and get a fire going. If we can not do that, the next best procedure is to locate as sheltered a spot as we can, curl up on something dry even though it be but spruce boughs or birchbark, and go to sleep.

You won't wake up? I'd heard the common admonition so often in New England that when I first went North I was apprehensive, also. But when the night turns cold at home, don't you awaken if only to reach for more covers? Cold also arouses you in the bush. You stir around just enough to get warm, which very often by changing position once or twice is all you do in bed, and then you draw yourself together again, go back to sleep if you can, or at least relax to the fullest extent possible.

This procedure can be especially important if we are short of food, as it stands to reason that the only way the body can produce the extra heat necessary to offset increased coldness is by burning additional calories. The supply of calories readily available for this function will be greatly lessened if we're also consuming them by tramping up and down.

The weaker one so becomes, the less able he will be to withstand what he is up against. When he slumps down exhausted, that is an entirely different situation, especially as there is probably perspiration to rob the clothing of an important part of its warmth. The reserve strength that would otherwise have been available is too many times depleted. From that sleep of exhaustion, there often is no awakening.

Another thing to beware when combating cold is alcohol. Although this may bring about a deceptive sensation of agreeable warmth, it has the effect of disrupting the function of the human thermostat, thereby drastically increasing in proportion to the amount consumed the possibility of serious effects resulting from exposure.

Snowslide

That anyone caught in a snowslide has a good chance to walk away from it is certain, especially if he can keep on top of the swirling and billowing avalanche. One way to accomplish this is by a swimming motion. The backstroke, particularly efficacious if it can be managed, has saved numerous lives in such emergencies.

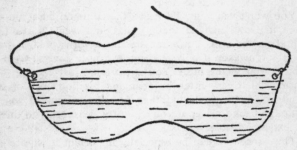

Fig. 65. Emergency goggles.

Snow Blindness

Snow blindness is a painful and watery inflammation of the eyes resulting from overexposure to certain light rays particularly when these are so diffused by water particles, frozen or otherwise, that they seem to strike the eyeball from every direction. The same symptoms result from exposure to glare from sand.

Treatment lies in avoiding all sunlight as much as possible. Eyes should be bandaged in a case of severe irritation, as the closed eyelids do not afford sufficient protection. This is true even inside a tent, as those of us who at some time have collected a sunburn through canvas can appreciate. Sourdoughs occasionally use cold weak tea to bathe the eyes when they first seem to be filled with harsh, gritty soap powder. Some find cold compresses of tea leaves soothing. Here, too, is where the antiseptic, anesthetic eye ointment suggested for the emergency aid kit will be really appreciated.

Snow blindness can be prevented by keeping excessive light from the eyes. The most convenient way of accomplishing this is with sunglasses. Large lenses, well fitted not too far from the face, are advisable because of the additional protection they afford from side glare.

Cheap sunglasses are usually fragile, seldom give sufficient eye protection at any time, are frequently uncomfortable, and are prone generally to have lens shortcomings and defects that may injure eyesight. Plastic is not recommended, particularly when replacement may be difficult, if only because of its susceptibleness to scratches and abrasions. Sunglasses that clip into place may damage regular glasses and, furthermore, do not exclude sufficient glare except from directly in front.

Eye protectors can be improvised from strips of wood or bone in which narrow slits have been cut. These have the advantage of not frosting under ordinary conditions. They have the disadvantage of severely restricting the vision. When the sun is high enough, shades such as those that can be fashioned from birchbark will help to cut down light, especially if their insides are darkened, perhaps with charcoal from the fire. Darkening about the eyes, as with soot, will also decrease reflected light.

Mire

We occasionally find dangerous quagmires where mud, decaying vegetation, or both are mixed with water in proportions not solid enough to support our weight.

That is all there is to it, for no inherent suction or evil influence exists within to draw one downwards, and as a matter of fact all that operates is gravity assisted by any unwise struggling. If you try to pull one of two imprisoned legs loose while taking all the resulting pressure on the other leg, the action will of course force this leg deeper.

At the worst, when you get very far into the mire your body will probably be lighter than the semisolid it displaces, and you will stop sinking. You will not go deeper, that is, unless you worm and twist your way down, trying ineffectually to get away. The thing to do, therefore, is to present as much body area to the surface of the mire as may be necessary and to do this with the utmost promptness.

A horse is caught quickly, for example, because of the comparative smallness of its feet, whereas a moose of similar weight will walk across the same quagmire without difficulty because of the way its hoofs spread apart to present a larger surface. The human foot is also a comparatively small area pressed downward by a correspondingly heavy weight.

If when you feel the instability you can get to solid land by running, that will be the end of the matter. If you cannot do this, fall to your knees, for you will generally be able to make it that way.

If you are still sinking, look around quickly to see if there isn't some branch or bush you can grab. Or you may have a pack or a coat to help support your weight. If not, flatten out on your stomach with your limbs as far apart as possible and crawl. You may have to do this, anyway.

One finds quagmires in all sorts of country. Areas where water remains on the surface, and particularly where water has so lain may be treacherous. We should watch out for tidal flats, swamps, marshes, old water holes which tremble beneath a topping of dried mud, and certainly for muskegs.

Quicksand

Quicksand is similar to quagmire, being sand that is suspended in water. It may drop you a whole lot more quickly, but methods of extrication are similar. You do not have as much time, however, and you're in more potential danger unless you keep your head.

Unless help is nearby or there is some support to grasp, you may be able to throw yourself immediately full length and either crawl or swim free. You may have to duck under water to loosen your feet, digging around with the hands and perhaps quickly sacrificing footwear. You will want to avoid as much as possible any sudden and abrupt motions that would only serve to shove you deeper.

Rest but do not ever give up, for quicksands and quagmires often occupy a hole no larger around than a sofa or large chair.

Although I have been fortunate enough never to be seriously caught myself, I once almost lost a saddle horse I was riding, when it spooked to one side, and on another occasion a pack horse. The first I had to pull out backwards, head over tail, with another cayuse, while the second wallowed to firm ground herself once freed of loaded paniers. In both widely separated places where my animals were bogged down, I was able to walk on sound footing close enough on every side to assure them with a hand.

Another inch or two of progress, in other words, may very well bring your fingers either to solidness or to where you can loop over a bush a belt or perhaps a rope made of clothing. If you can reach where vegetation is growing, you will almost certainly find sufficient support to allow you to get loose.

Chapter 23

Emergency Aid

AUTHOR'S NOTE: Thomas J. Gray, M. D., has kindly answered countless questions and offered numerous suggestions in connection with the medical information in Chapters 23 and 24; the responsibility for which, however, remains entirely the author's.

Realizing the potential vitalness of this subject to anyone in remote regions, Major Gray has given freely of innumerable evenings and weekends during the several years this book was in preparation, considering its possibilities and probabilities from what is the viewpoint of a qualified and experienced medical doctor who, widely experienced in isolated areas, also comprehends the peculiar problems of the farther places.

We both understand that no one can prescribe from a distance. Much of the data herein, in other words, should be considered not as any final dictum but, rather, as a time-saving meeting ground on which the individual may arrange for his particular needs with his own physician.

MAN IS a contrary critter. A lot of us are working harder than we want, at things we don't like to do. Why? It figures! In order to afford the sort of existence we don't care to live.

It also seems an odd thing, until you begin to analyze it, but an unhealthy proportion of accidents occur because down underneath someone wants them to happen. A mishap may be a face-saving excuse for some failure. Very often it is deliberately willed because the individual believes he should be punished. Occasionally someone has a misadventure because that's the easiest way to draw attention to himself. Now and then an accident offers the simplest escape from responsibility.

Once anybody definitely realizes that he cannot afford to have an accident, however, the percentages line up heavily against the probability of one overtaking him. This is especially noticeable in the wilderness, and logically so.

What would be a very minor incident in a city, with assistance as near as the telephone, could be an extremely serious and even fatal misstep in the farther places. So, both consciously and subconsciously, most humans are wholesomely careful to sidestep trouble when they are in remote areas. Away from the masses, too, one is not so apt to become entangled in the lapses and shortcomings of others.

All this is a major reason why among able-bodied men the probability of an accident or serious physical trouble in the deep wilderness is extremely small. In the comparative cleanliness of the silent places, furthermore, there is correspondingly little likelihood of infection. The exception to this latter circumstance has to do with the progressive lessening of built-up immunities while one is not in usual contact with the ills of civilization. This is a gradual matter and, being important only upon recontact, is at most a minor consideration unless one is to remain in remote country for a period of months or years.

What About Ready-Made Kits

Any one who goes over half a day from civilization and a doctor should whenever possible be armed with an adequate first-aid kit and a fair working knowledge of how to use it. This precaution he owes, at the very least, both to himself and to any who accompany him. No more than a reasonable measure, it can sometimes mean the difference between an easily repaired disability and one that lasts a lifetime.

The ready-packed commercial kits, excellent as they are

for many purposes, seldom are satisfactory for the individual who wanders far from beaten trails. One reason is that their assembly is based more or less on the assumption that the patient can be placed under a doctor's care within a comparatively brief period. Furthermore, these kits do not always include provisions for those accidents most likely to occur in wild country. As for the Army first-aid kit, this is designed for the emergency treatment of battle wounds.

It is not necessary that such an emergency-aid outfit be carried on the person, although it should be readily available at the camp, canoe, or other base of operations. Even a small and compact affair attached to the belt soon becomes an unwarranted nuisance, however, especially as at best one would be useful in no more than a disproportionate few of the emergencies that uncommonly occur. Something can always be extemporized on the spot to do for a short time. Even a functional splint, for example, can be improvised from a thick live roll of birchbark, peeled from a tree whose circumference is similar to that of the injured limb.

Snake Bite Kit

Taking up only slightly more space than one of the larger shotgun shells, one of the efficient little snake bite kits that can be easily tucked into a pocket should always be on the person in bad snake country. Especially handy are the Cutter Compak Suction Snake Bite Kits, each containing: three suction cups, a sharp blade, antiseptic, lymph constrictor, and a calmly presented completeness of plainly illustrated directions.

The four kinds of poisonous snakes in the United States are the rattler, coral, moccasin, and copperhead. The dangerousness of these is in general considerably overrated, mortality from properly treated snake bite being less than one per cent. Even without treatment of any sort, mortality only runs ten to fifteen per cent; hence the mistaken acclaim given such useless and often harmful "remedies" as tobacco juice, whiskey, kerosene, freshly killed fowl and, incidentally, the brilliant and effective looking potassium permanganate. Searing is likewise ineffectual and, except as it may in emergency be resorted to for stopping dangerous bleeding such as that caused by imprudent slashing, most definitely unwarranted.

Items for the Pocket

A flat metal or plastic container, taking up less space in a pocket than the ordinary folded handkerchief, will hold a small amount of aspirin and laxative. There will also be room, in case it is considered that you could one day need them, for a few dexedrine sulphate pills or some other concentrated stimulant suggested by your doctor—to be used only in a crisis when you, or someone else, might require additional sustained energy in a hurry. Common and usually adequate stimulants, if you have the makings on your person when you need them, are of course such caffeine-containing beverages as tea, coffee, and cocoa.

It is not a bad idea, either, to carry an antiseptic for emergency use on cuts and scratches. This may be in the form of several tiny bottlettes of Merthiolate or individual iodine applicators.

A few small, individually wrapped adhesive bandages scattered among the pockets are always coming in handy. The prompt use of one will, for example, ofttimes prevent chafing. You, too, have perhaps also employed these for repairing everything from clothing to knife sheaths.

Nothing can spoil an outdoor trip more surely than trouble with the feet. This usually unnecessary dilemma can often be relieved on the trail by the prompt use of the small ready-made gauze dressings centered on bits of adhesive tape and sold under various trade names. If you feel a spot starting to become tender, stop and cover it with as many of these preferably plain adhesive bandages as may be necessary. One is usually sufficient, as you will be able to tell best after you have started to walk again.

Frequently, the danger and the annoyance of blistering can thus be averted. Even after these vesicles have appeared, a properly applied dry dressing of this sort will many times prevent further friction and, left on, will allow the spot to harden. It is a mistake to cover a blistered heel with adhesive tape as many do, for healthful air is thus excluded and the area beneath is kept moist and soft without any chance to toughen. If there are already breaks in the skin, an infection has all the more opportunity to develop as we have seen happen on more than one occasion.

Personal Kit

A small but comprehensive emergency-aid kit should be no farther away than your outfit whenever you are in an area remote from medical coverage. This kit, whose composition will be largely an individual matter, should be adequate both for first aid and for those measures that may reasonably be necessary during the time it would take a doctor to contact a patient. It should contain, too, medications that you know from experience you may need personally.

How you pack such essentials will depend to a large degree on the way you travel. One method of keeping these items sterile and intact is to stow them in a tin can with a tightly fitting top. If it seems desirable, this cover may be reinforced with a strip of tape. For years, I've used a small red ditty bag that is convenient for hanging within reach and, at the same time, safely out of the way. This zippered red bag I enclose in a waterproof container when there is danger from dampness. Whenever rough handling becomes a hazard, I secure it within the protective softness of my eiderdown.

Depending on where you plan to go and on what may be your individual problems, your basic emergency aid kit may include some, most, or all of the articles listed in the table on the following pages.

Such a kit you can augment with salt and baking soda from the cooking outfit. Fill in with small adhesive bandages. Those with plastic tape adhere better. Plain and untreated little gauze pads are preferable, the ones medicated with antiseptics or antibiotics not being recommended. Add anything else that your experience indicates you will probably need or which your doctor recommends, perhaps after consideration of some of the possibilities mentioned in the following chapter.

BASIC EMERGENCY AID KIT

TAKE	FOR
1 triangular 40" sterile bandage (with 2 safety pins)	Direct application while sterile over wounds, covering sterile dressings, slings, padding, splint and traction ties, tourniquet
6 assorted gauze roller bandages of different widths in individual sterile packages 6 gauze compresses, 3" square, each in sterile packing	Direct application over wounds, direct pressure to stop bleeding, holding compresses in place
1 package small adhesive compresses with plastic tape and plain sterile pads	Cover minor wounds, tape abrasions to guard against irritation and infection, protect blisters, draw cuts together in field, etc.
1 small bar detergent	Cleanse hands before applying first aid, scrub wounds
50 or less aspirin tablets, 5-grain	Counteract pain, relieve shock, lower temperature
1 small applicator bottle fresh 2% tincture of iodine	Disinfect small wounds, paint tick bites, antiseptic
2 rolls adhesive tape, 2" wide	General taping, holding compress in place, emergency repairs
2 to 4 elastic bandages, 4" wide	Applied fully stretched over compress, one or more of these as may be necessary will usually control severe bleeding while, unlike the dangerous and temporary tourniquet, permitting circulation. Furthermore, these can be used anywhere, while tourniquets will serve only for the extremities. Even here, application will many times permit the gradual and fairly immediate removal of already applied tourniquet. Good for strapping chest tight to exclude air in puncture wounds, for bandaging of fractures and dislocations, for pressure bandages when applied at half stretch for strains and sprains

1 snake bite kit in country where it may be needed

In bad snake country, each individual should have a personal kit on his person at all times

¼-oz. tube of antiseptic-anesthetic eye ointment

Soothing and treating eye injuries and minor infections, deadening prior to removing embedded particle if distance makes this necessary, treatment of pain and irritation of snow blindness

1 good fever thermometer

Average normal temperature 98.6 fluctuations of one degree not usually being regarded as significant

1 small excellent scissors, pointed

In addition to regular uses, these can after sterilization be employed to spread in preference to slashing the incisions indicated in snake bite treatment. Such disruption of the tissue by blunt dissection, although painful, will more safely avoid injury to blood vessels, tendons, and nerves

1 sharply pointed tweezers or splinter forceps

Removing thorns and splinters. The latter may also be valuable in spreading open, rather than cutting, certain incisions

laxative

A supply of the brand you may prefer

2 curved surgeon's needles, with ligature and needle holder

For emergency sewing, when sterilized as by boiling, of wounds not easily closed by other means. Cleanse wound first, as by flushing liberally with sterile water. Pick out any debris and even scrub if that seems necessary. After sewing, paint externally with tincture of iodine

oil of cloves (or something else to treat toothache)

Dip bit of cotton in oil of cloves and insert in freshly cleaned cavity that is causing toothache. More modern treatments may well be favored by your doctor

Vitamins B Complex and C in high potency, stress doses

To replenish body needs being drained by severe accident or illness, which set up a condition of stress that very quickly depletes the body of certain vital substances, among which are the endocrines, which are extremely valuable in the successful resolution of such troubles. It is then important to maintain an adequate nutrition—emphasizing B complex, C, and protein—and these stress doses can mean the difference

1 first-aid guide (supplemented, as by marginal notes made with your doctor's help, with information about the additional steps that might become necessary in remote regions)

The terse, compact booklet on this subject put out by the United States Forest Service is excellent. It is available for 20 cents (stamps not accepted) from the Supt. of Documents, U.S. Govt. Printing Office, Washington 25, D.C.

Chapter 24

Backwoods Medicine

IF YOU are going into extreme wilderness, perhaps on a canoe or pack horse trip that will take you days and possibly weeks beyond the nearest physician, you may care to consult your personal doctor on the advisability of including for emergency use a vial of twenty 1/4 grain morphine sulphate hypo tablets to be procured and used as directed. These may be invaluable for such uses as counteracting pain, as when a frozen foot has been thawed and treated and when the victim is warm and protected, for combating shock, and for controlling severe digestive troubles as by breaking up a cycle of vomiting.

Better for administration in extreme shock, however, may be a box of five automatic injectors of morphine sulphate, sterilized and ready for instant use, or a smaller box of five collapsible-tube syringes of morphine tartrate, injected as directed.

Any of these preparations may be taken by placing loosely under the tongue where, not swallowed, it will be absorbed systemically into the general circulation, the effect of one dose usually lasting about four hours.

Duration and effect depend, of course, on the individual and the circumstances. In any event, similar dosage should be repeated only with the utmost care and caution and then ordinarily only once every four to six hours. A conservative procedure for the layman on his own is to hoard his supply sensibly, not using one until the need seems absolutely imperative.

Digestive Upsets

Ask your doctor, too, about a prescription of paregoric tablets for possible use in quieting the system after a severe digestive upset, once the body has had time to expel the causes. Primitive man was probably beset by few infectious food-carried maladies. Such diseases thrive only in crowded areas, and during those earlier eons there was no such unnatural crowding. You're not apt to have such trouble when alone in the bush, therefore, but you can very easily contract it on the way to the jumping off spot.

If you stop at any doubtful or overbusy eating places, it will be wise neither to drink water there nor to order cold or raw food. It will be best, too, to eat only meat that is well done all the way through. Ground meat can be especially dangerous. Safest choices are bottled soft drinks, black tea made on the spot with boiling water, and thoroughly and freshly cooked foods served hot from the kitchen.

Food Poisoning

In severe food poisoning verging on collapse, one treatment is to wash out the stomach with a weak solution of sodium bicarbonate, ¼ teaspoon to a glass of cool water. Drink two glasses of this right on top of each other. This may be vomited, or it may pass right through. Sometimes nothing else is necessary except, perhaps, a restricted diet of weak tea and dry toast for the next day.

If the trouble does continue, it will be necessary to retard the intensity of the bowel movements so as to permit the building up of a concentration of medication. One way to accomplish this former is with paregoric which can be conveniently carried in outdoor kits in the form of tiny 10-minim tablets, of which a vial of twenty-four occupies only a very small space. An adult might take two or three of these tablets every four to six hours for as long as the need continues. If there were a moderate recurrence of diarrhea after a four hour period, for instance, one or two more tablets might do. The desired effect is, of course, only symptomatic; that is, paregoric combats not the cause but the digestive irritability.

Vomiting at the onset might pose a problem. The individual might be able to hold down the initial dose of paregoric long enough for sufficient to be absorbed to check the vomiting. Otherwise, the cycle could be broken by holding under the tongue until absorbed a ¼-grain morphine sulphate hypo tablet or the released contents of one of the previously mentioned automatic injectors or collapsible-tube syringes.

The trouble itself could then be attacked by one of the largely non-soluble sulfas. Incidentally, the formerly widely recommended purge of calomel or some similar purgative, is no longer generally approved, the feeling being that sufficient action of this sort will have probably already ensued, and that taking a cathartic will therefore be sort of like whipping a jaded horse.

Your doctor, as of this writing, may suggest that you include in your outfit two or three dozen one-half gram tablets of sulfathalidine or sulfaguanidine. You could then take four tablets of either.

If the trouble continued, you might reasonably assume:

(1) either the medication is not hitting,
(2) or it hasn't reached the affected area,
(3) or there is not sufficient concentration.

Normally, two more tablets could then be repeated in 4 to 6 hours. If these still don't act, two more could be repeated in another 4 to 6 hours. In the bush you might give three or four tries, then go to something else such as penicillin if that were available.

Once cured, it is often well to stay pretty much on light rations such as weak tea and toast for a day, while replenishing in repeated small amounts of slightly salted water the often critically depleted fluid level of the body, dehydration and salt depletion being major dangers in such upsets.

Penicillin

Penicillin can now be taken orally and be just as effective if not more so than shots administered intramuscularly, which is why your doctor may suggest your taking along a supply of oral penicillin, perhaps in combination with one or more of the safer sulfa drugs. Because of their qualities of absorption, some of these penicillin compounds should as directed be taken before meals. A bottle of fifty tablets does not occupy much room. The standard tablet contains about 250,000 units of penicillin, the average dose for infection with fever then being one tablet, four to six hours apart, three or four times a day.

In case of pneumonia, to give an example, a not unusual treatment would be one tablet three or four times a day as directed. This would be continued until there was a definite response—a clinical improvement, that is, particularly the all important one signified by the dropping of fever. This is a reason why a good thermometer belongs in the first aid kit. As soon as the temperature remained normal for twelve hours, the dosage might be halved for two days. A reason for not stopping it immediately is that when the infection is not adequately treated but only suppressed, it may flare up again.

If some infection were likely as a result perhaps of a bad cut, a sound preventative step might be to go on half dosage for three days. A more serious situation, as in the instance of a compound fracture, would call for full dosage. Penicillin is known to have some effect in combating tetanus. It might be preventatively used, therefore, if there seemed to be even a remote possibility of tetanus as from a gunshot wound or from a deep puncture wound contaminated by soil, clothing, or anything else.

It is not advisable to take antibiotics for long periods. A week is usually long enough. If there is no response by then, the particular antibiotic is probably doing no good and may as well be quit anyway. Antibiotics when effective work only on a secondary mathematical basis. That is, they hold down the multiplication of foreign bacteria and thus permit the system to gain the upper hand by marshaling its own forces of resistence.

Bleeding

The commonest outdoor injuries are cuts followed by sprains and strains, bruises, and then fractures. Hands and fingers are hurt most often, then feet and toes, and next legs. One out of every four injuries coming to the attention of the U. S. Forest Service is caused by hand tools such as axes and knives. These latter are the most immediately serious whenever accompanied by heavy bleeding, for this must be stopped at the earliest possible second. Even where a severed artery is no larger than the graphite in a pencil, an individual can last for no more than a few minutes at most if its bleeding is not checked.

Pressing a clean and preferably sterile dressing over the wound will usually control the bleeding if sufficient pressure is applied. This usually can be done, especially with the assistance if necessary of elastic bandages used as previously described. If not, press firmly and strongly against the nearest pressure point. The blood supply to an entire arm can be shut off by pressing just behind the ridge to be felt on the inner side of the armpit beneath the raised arm.

The large femoral artery of the leg can be controlled by gripping the leg near the body and drawing the fingers about halfway down the inner surface where they will find a slight depression at whose bottom throbs this great arterial trunk. Incidentally, the blood vessels of the lower leg can often be closed by pressing under the flexed knee between the two major tendons in that area.

If the bleeding still continues dangerously, the next step is to apply a tourniquet to the elevated limb. Any preferably flat wide material will do for this, but particularly efficacious is a resilient two-inch-wide rubber strip, about five feet long, which may be cut from a live inner tube and carried for possible emergency use.

Once the bleeding is stopped by the tourniquet, it will be necessary if medical assistance is not within easy reach to control the wound so that the tourniquet, which otherwise would cause gangrene, may be taken off or at least loosened once every twenty minutes. Elastic bandages applied at full stretch over compresses will now usually permit cautious removal of the tourniquet. After allowing time for the blood to clot in the gauze, loosen the tourniquet slowly until assured of the effects, controlling it like a turn-off valve.

There is also the Spartan but effectual procedure of a harsher age—the stoppage of bleeding by the searing of the wound, as with the blade of a knife heated red-hot in a campfire.

Breath Stoppage

Immediate action is necessary whenever breathing stops as a result of smoke inhalation, drowning, or electric shock as from lightning.

Place victim face downwards with feet higher than head. Loosen clothing. Bend elbows and place hands one atop the other. Turn face to side, chin up, cheek upon hands. Check mouth and make sure air passage is not blocked. If tongue has been swallowed, hook it free with a forefinger.

Kneel on one or both knees at victim's head, facing him. Place heels of hands just below line between arm pits; thumb tips touching, fingers downward and outward.

Rock forward on straight elbows, with steady pressure on victim's back. Rock backward, sliding hands to other's arms just above elbows. Grasp arms, continuing to rock backward. Raise arms until tension is felt, then lower arms.

This completes the cycle, which should be repeated twelve times a minute for several hours if necessary. Once victim has been revived, treat for shock. If possible, keep victim lying comfortably in a quiet and warm place for twenty-four hours.

Fractures

Wilderness procedure in case of fracture must often continue far beyond ordinarily recommended first aid practices which, however, should whenever it is feasible be adhered to as closely as practicable.

It is often possible to make one's own way to help by splinting a broken leg sufficiently to immobilize the region of the break, slinging the leg up out of the way, and then proceeding with the help of a crotched stick cut as a crutch. Particular caution should always be taken not to shut off circulation, frequent re-examinations being made as the injury swells.

If you were alone in deserted country where it seemed imperative actually to set a leg, the first step would be to secure the foot as by tying it to a tree. You would then have to apply traction, perhaps by pulling on another tree with a crooked arm. This you would do very slowly, attempting to reduce the fracture by persistent pressure rather than by any sudden yank. You might be able to help by shoving with your free foot, all the time trying to align the broken ends with the fingers of one hand. Muscle spasms usually set up a terrific pressure, but this may be capitalized upon later to help hold the bones in place.

Dislocations

It is sometimes necessary in remote areas to attempt to set a dislocation you'd ordinarily leave for the doctor. A friend of mine, swept off his horse in thick Northern timber, got a dislocated hip back into place by tying his leg to a poplar and pulling with both arms on another sapling.

If a companion dislocates a shoulder, it may be reduced by having the victim lie down while you sit beside him and place a bared foot in his armpit. Pull the dislocated arm out slowly and steadily at right angles, turning it carefully from side to side. So handled, it will often slip gently and easily back through the original ligamentous tear.

If possible immobilize and rest reduced dislocations for several weeks, making sure at all times that subsequent swelling does not cut off circulation, for this, as can be appreciated, can result in far greater trouble than any difficulties brought on by the dislocation. Indications of a too tightly bandaged arm, for example, are numb, cold, tingly, or blue fingers.

Infected Wounds

For a local infection, in addition to first aid open and drain. For an infection that extends over a wide area, apply hot compresses or soak in hot brine in an effort to localize it.

For actual or threatened infection in the critical facial triangle, the base of which extends above the eyebrows and the apex of which encloses the lips, treat with continuously renewed hot packs. Do not squeeze at any time. Do not even attempt to lance until the infection becomes so extremely localized that it can be easily opened with a sterile needle.

A felon occasionally must be widely opened. The raw lining of an egg shell makes an effective poultice. A functional way to provide suction is by heating an open bottle which, applied over the felon, will draw as it cools.

Antibiotics, as suggested elsewhere, should be considered in connection with infections. If an individual happened to be stranded without medicine and with an infection that was not responding to treatment, he might in a pinch elect to eat any bread, cheese, or similar rations covered with green mold—this with the hope of introducing penicillin into the system. In critical circumstances when not even such mold was available, some doctors believe it might be worthwhile as a desperate resort to try eating small amounts of dirt in the hope of thus obtaining life-saving antibiotics.

Poisonous Snake Bite

Keep as quiet and calm as possible, thereby avoiding to the greatest possible degree any unnecessary quickening of the circulation which would speed absorption of the poison into the general system.

Tie a band 1½ inches above both bite and swelling if possible to restrict the flow of the lymph vessels and veins. A handkerchief, torn strip of clothing, or lace will serve. This is *not* a tourniquet, nor should that be applied. Loosen a bit if the limb numbs or becomes cold. Remove band for a minute about every ten minutes. Continue if you can to reapply slightly higher.

Clean the skin as well as possible where any cutting is to be done, so as not to complicate the situation by introducing germs or dirt into these wounds. If tincture of iodine is at hand, paint with that, or wash with detergent or soap if this can be done with a minimum of delay.

If nothing better is available, sterilize the point of your knife blade in a fire or over a match flame. Then make a ¼ inch cross to or slightly beyond the depth of the bite through each fang mark.

During all cutting, be extremely careful to avoid arteries, tendons, nerves, and large veins. Because of the very real dangers all these impose, safer although more painful than slashing is the spreading and working of the tissue apart with the sterilized points of scissors or, even better, splinter forceps. Cut the skin just enough to allow entry of the points. The tissue beneath the skin can also be parted and disrupted with a single bluntish end.

Apply suction to the incisions. Lacking a suction pump or cups, suck and spit out blood and venom. A warmed bottle will as it cools also provide suction. If you can do nothing better, press and squeeze out blood and venom.

Ticks

Some ticks especially in certain areas carry Rocky Mountain spotted fever, an infection formerly more dangerous than it is now. Immunization with spotted fever vaccine is sometimes used as a preventative. Chloromycetin and aureomycin have been found to control this heretofore too often fatal fever within one day.

Ticks are usually only annoyances, fortunately. Penetration of an egg-heavy female at the base of the skull can be dangerous, however, especially as she is apt to remain hidden in the hair until perhaps an increasing stiffness of the neck causes a close inspection. If all parts of the tick are not found and removed, respiratory paralysis and even death are serious possibilities.

What can be developing into a bothersome tick bite may be lanced one-eighth of an inch deep and suction applied for twenty minutes. A hot salt or wet grain poultice, if not too irritating to the individual, may help if left on from half to three-quarters of an hour. You can also apply some antiseptic such as fresh two percent tincture of iodine, allow to dry, cover with a sterile compress, and bandage.

An antihistamine ointment affords relief to many if applied early enough and if sensitivity exists. At the discretion of your doctor, inclusion of a few antihistamines for specific allergies such as poison oak, and for any aid they might give in the alleviation of burns, might well be warranted.

Ticks generally do not dig their heads in and begin to suck blood for a few hours and can be detected by daily afternoon inspection and removed by sliding a keen knife between them and your epidermis. The heat from a match or ember will encourage them to back out from the body, as will touching them with coal oil, gasoline, or something alcoholic even though it's only shaving lotion.

Trying to pull or to unscrew them reversely or otherwise unless as with adequately applied tweezers which do not kill the tick is not so good, sometimes leaving parts of the head behind to cause irritation if not serious infection. Ticks should never be crushed during removal. Even after they have been taken off uninjured, the common technique of squashing them with the fingers is dangerous because of thus released organisms that may be absorbed by the human system. Tossing them into the campfire will explode them instantaneously.

Eye Ointment

If back in the bush anything becomes lightly embedded in the cornea, that transparent outer coating of the eye through which light is admitted to the iris and pupil, it can soon become so unbearable that if skilled medical assistance is days away some careful local action may be warranted. This is one reason for including in the kit a small tube of an antiseptic and anesthetic eye ointment suggested by your doctor, which will be of potential value, too, in soothing an irritated eye or treating a superficial infection. A possibility, for example, is a $\frac{1}{4}$ ounce tube of 2% Butyn and Metaphen.

In the above instance, first deaden the eye by using the ointment as directed. Then sterilize a needle. Fire will accomplish this, and if you keep the tip in the blue portion of a match flame, carbon will not form. If there is any remaining blackness, however, wipe the point clean with something sterile such as cotton dipped in tincture of iodine. This is particularly important, as otherwise an obscuring fleck of black might be left in the cornea.

Approach the foreign body very cautiously and steadily from the side with the sterile needle, holding it parallel to the eye rather than point first. Very often the object can thus be touched at its edge and flicked out, much in the fashion of playing tiddlywinks.

Oddments

There are other odds and ends that you may want to put in the emergency aid kit, as for example something such as mentholated salve for chapped lips. Items available elsewhere in the outfit can frequently be made to perform double duty, however.

Half a teaspoon of salt in a glass of water is medically regarded as equal to commercial mouthwashes. No larger a proportion of salt should be used than one-half of a level teaspoon to every glass of water, for when a solution is employed that is stronger in salt than the body fluid, its tendency is to draw natural moisture out of the body, dehydrating tissue and causing irritation.

Baking soda, the medical and dental professions assure us, is as good a dentifrice as most and far less expensive than any of the manufactured products.

A paste of baking soda and water applied on insect stings

and bits will often help reduce the swelling and irritation. Soaking in water when possible is even simpler. Daubing on mud will do, too, in a pinch. The itching from hives, skin irritation caused by chafing, allergies, and so on, can often be relieved by patting on a paste of baking soda and water or by applying bandages or compresses soaked in a saturated solution of this same sodium bicarbonate.

For indigestion ¼ teaspoon of baking soda in ½ glass of water, not to be repeated more than two or three times any day and definitely not to be used habitually, often helps ease the discomfort of acid indigestion and heartburn. If the necessity for an antacid is prolonged, one of the inert alkalies should be used instead of sodium bicarbonate. One-half teaspoon of baking soda in a glass of water will serve as a gargle or mouthwash.

Plain ordinary table salt, a rounded teaspoon in a quart of warm water taken preferably before breakfast or at any rate on an empty stomach will serve as a purge. So in the wilderness will often a similar amount of cold spring water enjoyed while one is washing up the first thing in the morning.

Chapter 25

Survival Kit

How READY WE may be to meet the challenges of living off the country cannot help but depend to some extent upon how immediate the possibility of being so compelled may seem to us.

Some already have compact survival outfits packed, and with atom bomb havoc and the even more insidious carnage of man-loosed pestilence certainly not decreasing menaces, who can say that these perhaps more foresighted individuals are not actually being ultraconservative?

Many of us in any event find it reasonable to carry some sort of survival kit whenever traveling, for planes are still forced down in uninhabited regions, watercraft both great and small continue to be wrecked, while automobiles and entire trains are stalled with alarming persistency by accident, storm, and disaster.

The most casual of strollers, campers innumerable, vacationists, and continually surprising proportions of this continent's more than thirty million annually licensed hunters and fishermen keep on losing their ways by the tens of thousands. Numerous others are thrown upon their own resources by being unexpectedly stranded in remote regions; often, it should be added, because putting their own welfare last, they decline to leave distressed companions.

Emergency Kit

What, depending on its size, should such an emergency outfit logically contain? Most of us will at least want matches, compass, knife, mirror, maps, and, in addition to the several items each of us uses everyday, a few small adhesive bandages.

We may want to add such other articles as the right kind of firearm and ammunition, the most satisfactory type of ax, sharpening stone, rolled saw blade, fishhooks and line, safety pins, fly dope, adhesive tape, binoculars or small light telescope, flashlight, a few short stout candles, small magnifying glass, halazone tablets, rectangle of plastic for overhead waterproofing, sunglasses, and if prescription lenses are necessary certainly an extra pair.

It is possible we will desire to go farther and include extra clothing, toilet articles, a tarpaulin or light fly-proof tent, a carefully filled repair kit, light eiderdown sleeping robe, air mattress, canvas bucket, nested cooking outfit, canteen, and a few books—perhaps even this volume.

We may spend some time choosing a few pounds of the best possible emergency foods. And how about our first aid kit?

Quality

An axiom to be followed with painstaking nicety when selecting the composites of any survival kit is to procure the best we can afford. A poor knife, for example, can be expected to weigh as much as a good one. It is very apt to weigh more because of extra material needed to reinforce it and as a result of ornamentation designed to draw attention from more obvious shortcomings. When we're really up against it for a blade, the supposed bargain may fail us.

"There is hardly anything in the world that some men cannot make a little bit worse and sell a little cheaper," said John Ruskin, "and the people who consider price only are this man's lawful prey."

Cost cannot of course be considered to be necessarily the final indicator of desirability one way or the other. As a matter of fact, the expensive extras sometimes supplementing otherwise functional merchandise may add for our purposes unwarranted bulk and weight. The soundest precautions to take when in doubt are, as many of us do: to ascertain as many facts as possible, to weigh them as finely as we can on the scales of our own individual requirements, and finally to trade with a reliable and an experience dealer.

The Way to Compromise

Certain equipment, into which category such items as sleeping robes often fall, may cost more than some of us may rightly wish to expend at the moment. The wisest compromise in such an event is not, to continue the example, the selection of a cheap heavy sleeping contraption that will never prove satisfactory. Much better will be the selection of a good woolen blanket or two and, if you like the bag arrangement, a half-dozen horse blanket pins.

The Problems of Packing

A number of small, differently colored cloth bags will help keep the various elements of a survival kit in order. Such containers can be made easily enough at home so as to close either with draw strings or with slide fasteners. Tying a rawhide loop through a reinforced corner of each will enable its being hung conveniently nearby in camp, perhaps on a limb trimmed so as to leave a few handy projections and stuck by the head of the bed.

Each of us will gradually work out a system best suited to his own needs, perhaps along the lines of my acquired habit of keeping medicinals in a red sack, repair items in a green, writing and reading supplies in a grey, handkerchiefs and shorts in a brown, and stockings in a long dark container whose shade does not matter as it can be located by feel. The toilet kit I use daily consists of a small rubberized bag for wet articles, fitting within a larger oilskin sack into which also go towel and such. I've found it a sound practice, too, to wrap and tie binoculars and all else that may be injured by dampness in individual slightly inflated waterproof coverings.

Everything I pack within a water repellent bag, distributing extra clothing so as to protect the more fragile essentials.

Stowing the Survival Kit

It may be advantageous, if the outfit is small enough, to arrange it in a garment that has no purpose except to support a large number of pockets. Such an arrangement is the Emergency Sustenance Vest of the U. S. Army Air Forces, obtainable at some surplus retailers.

The vest, which is adjustable to the individual's size, affords no less than seventeen pockets whose substantial flaps are firmly securable with generally two snaps. This volume on survival, incidentally, will fit comfortably in the right inside compartment.

Only Two Packs Satisfactory

For a larger outfit you may want to secure a pack, especially as long ago you have probably learned the inadvisability of tiring one's self needlessly by awkwardly weighing down belts and pockets not designed for the purpose, and as you no doubt subscribe as well to the general rule never to carry anything in the hands that can be toted on the back.

Those who have had many years of packing experience, who have studied the problem, and who have been fortunate enough to be able to test the best available equipment have found that there are only two types of packs really satisfactory for all-day back packing—as differentiated from freight carries such as those across portages and to base camps.

The best in some ways, and certainly the more accessible of

the two, is the frame rucksack of the Bergans type. This design which can be recognized by its series of pockets and holding straps, is built around a large central pouch and supported against a light frame of metal tubing. This frame is held coolly and welcomely from the back by means of straps or webbing, so rigged that the load scarcely touches the body.

There is, therefore, a constant air circulation between the impedimenta and the back. You have to lug the customary shapeless, bulging packsack for awhile to appreciate fully the tremendous premium in comfort and in increased agility that this balance and ventilation represent.

The pack board, the other suitable type of pack, is what is preferred by a large number of trappers and prospectors. It will, incidentally, carry unbelievably heavy loads. Hard and unwieldly articles ranging from bags of quartz samples to outboard motors are commonly transported on it without bruising the back. There is no better article with which a man can bring out a sectioned moose.

The pack board consists of a light wooden or fiber frame over which a canvas cover is doubled and tightly laced and to which broad shoulder straps are attached. There is about a two and one-half inch air space between the two sides of taut canvas. The packer's sensation is not unlike that of a cool canvas cot being pressed against his back. Everything to be carried is wrapped ordinarily in some cover such as a tarpaulin, useful in camp, and lashed to the back of the pack board.

The pack board is comfortable, functional, less expensive than the frame rucksack, more adaptable in many ways, capable of being built without too much trouble by the individual, and is therefore very popular among both amateur and professional woodsmen. To get at anything in the pack en route, however, you must undo the entire load.

Both of these packs should be carried *not* high, but with the shoulder straps let out sufficiently to allow the pack to sag down slightly almost to the hips, until the pressure is brought to bear almost completely on the top rather than on the front of the shoulders.

Duffel Bag

Under many circumstances a duffel bag is convenient, particularly one that instead of being secured at the throat opens along its entire length, permitting the selection of whatever is wanted at the moment without a lot of disarranging and unpacking.

Such a duffel bag, which should be water resistant, will last for years of heavy usage, although if the fastening is one of the slide type it may have to be renewed. It is a good idea to obtain a bag that can be locked shut, not that this will exclude anyone who is determined to get at the contents, but it will thwart ordinary tampering. Handiest for locking the thing will be a padlock that is opened by the correct dialing of a combination, thus doing away with any need for keys. Such a duffel bag may well have at least one carrying strap that can be slipped over a shoulder for transporting the load short distances.

H. B. C. Emergency Kit

The Hudson's Bay Company, drawing upon nearly 300 years of experience in the wild places, has prepared a watertight emergency kit particularly for use on the trading concern's aircraft. This eleven-pound outfit, which is capable of floating, measures twelve inches by eleven inches by three and one-half inches.

The contents have been assembled with a view of maintaining one individual normally for one week. If the user cuts exertion and hardship to a minimum, the Hudson's Bay Company with characteristic conservatism estimates that the sustenance can be stretched about four times as far.

Provisions for signaling, lighting fires, cooking, fishing, catching birds, and snaring animals are among those made by this world's oldest trading corporation, once given by royal charter a large portion of the North American continent. Here is what the Governor and Company of Adventurers of

England trading into Hudson's Bay choose to include, and the reasons why:

Item	Quantity	Purpose
Tea Bags	28	Making of tea
Vitamin Pills	50	Making up for diet deficiency
Pilot Bread	30 oz.	Food
Butter	16 oz.	Food
Strawberry Jam	14½ oz.	Food
Klik	12 oz.	Food
Condensed Milk	14 oz.	Food
Chocolate Bars	10.5 oz.	Food
Matches	100	Lighting of fires
Knife	1	Multiple purposes
Spoon	1	Eating, fish bait, scoop, or shovel, etc.
Whistle	1	Signaling
Double-faced mirror	1	Signaling
Fishing line	1	Fishing, snaring, wick, string, etc.
Fishhooks	4	Fishing, catching birds
Snare Wire	1 oz.	Setting snares and various other uses
Candles	2	Cooking, light, etc.
Kleenex	Small amt.	Multiple purposes
Camphor		Mosquito bites, cuts, chapped lips.

The Science of Going Light

"It is some advantage to lead a primitive life if only to learn what are the necessaries," Thoreau found. "Most of the luxuries and many of the so-called comforts are not only dispensable but positive hindrances."

Chapter 26

Being Ready

THE PLEASURE to be derived from any excursion into the farther regions—and it is one of the peculiarities of human nature that the hardest and most disagreeable trips become the milestones by which outdoor careers are later most pleasantly measured—may be divided into three parts: the zest of getting ready, the enjoyment of remembering, and the journey itself.

Many contend that of these joys not the least is the anticipation, the thrill of planning, the excitement of thumbing books and catalogues, and the stimulus of adding and occasionally even subtracting from lists with stubby pencils kept handy for whenever inspiration fires.

As each of us observes the world from a different seat, it is only natural that points of view will vary on lesser and in some instances even on major items to be included in a personal survival kit. But that need be no reason for dissension, for as Colonel Townsend Whelen says, "I do not, for a minute, suppose my ways are the best ways, but at least it may be helpful to know the other fellow's points."

First Come Matches

Although fires may as we have considered be lit by several primitive methods, this can be accomplished neither so surely nor so easily that many will care to go into the bush without a waterproof case filled with long wooden matches. Most of us will probably agree, too, on the advisability of carrying an unbreakable container that can be fastened to the clothing and of keeping a second filled case handy as a spare. In the outfit itself, we may also want one or more watertight receptacles holding a reserve supply.

Then the Compass

The second thing the majority of us will not want to be without, despite the numerous natural ways we know indicate direction, is a compass. Nor will we disagree that it is a conservative precaution in this instance as well both to wear a compass pinned or tied to the clothing and also to take along a spare, and that at least one of these should have a luminous dial that can be consulted in the dark.

Adhesive Bandage

These little gauze pads centered on brief strips of adhesive tape are useful in such a variety of ways that one always seems to be finding employment for them if a few are kept in the pocket whenever in the wilderness, and if this is so, an additional supply certainly belongs in the survival kit. These should be left in the sterile wrappings in which most arrive, especially as these coverings have a secondary value in preventing dust and lint from robbing the tape of sticking power.

Plain bandages are rated best. Those treated with Mercurochrome and other medicaments have no properties that make them superior to ordinary pads, many doctors and laboratories hold. These sources contend further that such medication may even be detrimental. Plastic tape is an improvement over fabric, however, adapting itself more easily and often more substantially to various surfaces.

Prompt use of an inexpensive adhesive bandage the moment part of the foot begins to feel tender will many times prevent formation of a blister and a subsequent dangerous infection. Inasmuch as air will reach the affected area insofar as the bandage is concerned if the latter is properly applied, the dressing may be left on a day or so until the skin toughens. Adhesive bandages also prove convenient for divers other uses in the bush such as temporarily repairing clothing, fishing gear, binoculars, and even ax handles.

Glasses

Anyone who needs glasses will be prudent to carry an extra pair on the person and, advisedly, another pair in the survival outfit. In most country, it is a good idea to have along at least one pair of optically correct and ruggedly constructed sunglasses in a protective case.

Watch

A watch we find useful both because distances back of beyond are measured more often by time than by miles, and because a timepiece can be used under proper conditions to tell direction.

Map

Maps, which come under the heading of necessities for intelligent wilderness travel, are inexpensively and under ordinary circumstances easily obtainable, many being securable merely for the asking. A list of sources is given in an earlier part of this book.

Mirror

It is not uncommon to get foreign matter in the eyes if the bush is at all thick or if one is traveling, for example, along a river whose cut banks are almost constantly eroded by the wind. Under such conditions, one will have frequent use for a mirror, and there is the further fact that this mirror can be vital when it comes to attracting help in an emergency.

Magnifying Glass

A magnifying lens can be used during favorable weather to start a fire, either when no quicker means is available or when it may be desirable to conserve matches. One often comes in handy for odd functions, too, such as locating an embedded thorn or splinter.

Knives

While a pocket knife with a single thin blade will admittedly serve many purposes including the dressing out of the largest North American game animals, most will find it practical to add a sheath knife for the heavier tasks. A light blade five or six inches long works well for cutting boughs, blazing, preparing meat, securing some fuel, building shelters, and performing other tasks in the bush. A substantial and well riveted sheath should be added for safety.

Ax

Although for ordinary camping and hunting both the hatchet and belt ax have their merits, a more desirable tool for possible survival use is the Hudson Bay ax with its weight-lessening narrow butt. A one-and-one-half pound head on a twenty-four inch handle will enable one to put up a satisfactory log cabin in a pinch.

This does not mean that a larger and heavier tool will not be far more convenient if the moment comes when we need an ax. Whether the additional bulk and heft will be justified, particularly if its inclusion means the elimination of something else, must be a matter of individual decision. If a riveted leather sheath is not included with any ax that is selected, the cutting surface should be safely wrapped in something such as stout canvas.

Saw

Indians used to make saws of bone and of stone, and with good reason, for one can work up firewood much more swiftly and facilely with a saw designed for the purpose than with any ax, and with much less risk.

Inclusion of a Swede saw in the survival outfit will be, certainly, a worthwhile precaution. The thin narrow blade can be held in a compact roll by string wound among its large set teeth which when packed should be covered if only by rolling a section of canvas around them.

A two-piece tubular handle adds little weight and, when disjointed, not very much bulk. A handle may later be improvised on the spot, however, by bending a green sapling like a bow. Once the correct length has been estimated, the ends can be split and a single hole made through each with a knife, nail, etc. The handle can then be rebent, and the blade inserted and secured by twisted nails or by tying. Two butterfly bolts will make this latter function even simpler.

Carborundum

A small carborundum stone, coarse on one side and fine on the other, may be carried in the pocket to keep knife as well as other edged tools sharp. Although about the best way to accomplish this there are radically different opinions, perhaps you have also just naturally gravitated into the procedure found practical throughout the years by the dean of the outdoor writers, Colonel Townsend Whelen.

"Put a few drops of oil or water on the stone, lay the blade flat on it; if it is a pocket knife raise the back of the blade about $\frac{1}{8}$ inch off the stone, or for a broad-bladed sheath knife about $\frac{1}{4}$ inch. Keep the blade at this angle while sharpening.

"Pressing with medium weight on the blade, grind the edge with a circular movement, about thirty seconds on one side. Tilt the blade a little to grind the blade up toward the point. After a few minutes of grinding, it will be quite sharp but will have a featheredge. Then push the edge of the blade straight forward across the stone several times, turn it over and press the other side forward, and the featheredge will double and come off.

"The knife is then sharp enough for most purposes," concludes the Colonel. "If you want to shave with it, finish by stropping it on the soft leather of your boot top."

Gun and Ammunition

The most valuable survival weapon for living off the North American continent for an indefinite period is, for the reasons previously considered at length, a light and flat-shooting repeating rifle. Cartridges should be selected for meat-getting efficiency. If two or three firearms are to be carried by a party, all ideally should be similar so that the parts of any can be used to keep at least one functioning.

Sleeping Provisions

Eiderdown is the lightest and warmest material obtainable for the manufacture of sleeping robes. Down from other fowl ranks next. Feathers, types and desirability of which vary greatly, are in comparison bulky.

Snaps are for two reasons preferable to slide fastenings for use on sleeping robes:

(a) it is much easier with snaps to moderate the inside temperature of a robe,

(b) slide fasteners on such equipment have a tendency in all climates to get out of order, and in cold regions this then perhaps hazardous predicament may be the result of freezing.

For those who may like a small pillow, the better rubberized and plastic affairs which can be inflated by the mouth are convenient. When one is traveling too light to take an air mattress, such a pillow can be used to soften a broad shallow hip hole or to cushion a shoulder hole.

Tent or Tarp

To carry for possible emergency use, a tent will ordinarily be preferable to a tarpaulin only if there may be a serious need to exclude insects. Such a tent would be a small, light, flyproof model. A small tarp will otherwise prove more adaptable, cheerful, and efficient.

If the survival kit is small, one may very well settle for a rectangle of plastic, perhaps eight feet by four, which can be folded and carried in a shirt pocket. This will afford a waterproof roof which is the hardest thing to come by in any makeshift shelter.

Flashlight

When we boys camped at Lake Winnepesaukee and climbed nearby Mt. Shaw, we somehow got started one New Hampshire night auctioning off various oddments from our small outfits. An item that nobody who was lucky enough to have one along even offered to part with was a flashlight. That I remember, for mine had somehow become broken, and I was ready to bid high for a spare.

The two-cell flashlight is usually enough, preferably one with rounded lines that are not so prone to wear holes. A spare bulb, cushioned in cotton batting, can often be stowed in the end. It is a good idea to take along in the outfit an additional spare, perhaps inside a box of adhesive bandages. You will probably want at least two extra batteries.

The batteries will last much longer if the light is snapped on for only very brief periods at a time. An occasional flash is all that is needed, for example, while hiking at night. It is a sound precaution when packing to insert paper between batteries and bulb, for even securing the switch with tape does not always prevent the wasting of power accidentally.

Whistle

A whistle can be useful for attracting help, sending messages, keeping a group together, and for any other purposes when it will serve better than a shout. When a group goes out together, an often conservative precaution is to agree on a simple code, put it down on paper, and furnish each individual a copy to carry on his person.

Binoculars and Telescope

Either binoculars or telescope can be a far more important part of the survival kit than is generally appreciated; for locating landmarks, scouting out the most desirable routes, and certainly for securing meat.

Insect Repellent

Having a supply of one of the more effective fly dopes in the emergency kit can prevent a lot of misery during seasons when winged pests are prevalent in sometimes death-dealing multitudes.

Fishing Gear

This is something that you can have a lot of enjoyment with too, at unexpected times. Why not get a small metal box if you want, perhaps one of the flat pill containers, and fit in a few hook and flies? You might add some tiny strips of lead to be later twisted into place as sinkers, and you won't forget to wind a quantity of small durable fish line, such as nylon, on perhaps a piece of cardboard. You can always cut a pole. Safety pins, incidentally, can be made to serve as guides.

Writing Materials

You might bring some good light paper, a few envelopes perhaps, and a pencil or ball-point fountain pen. These will make it easier to leave any messages, one precaution that anyone lost should ordinarily take before leaving any emergency camp. Such materials may also be welcomed for mapping and for otherwise profitably passing the time.

Water Purifier

The tiny two-ounce bottles each holding one hundred halazone tablets take up little room and afford good insurance against impure drinking water. These minute tablets work by releasing chlorine gas and therefore should be fresh. A full bottle sells for about fifty cents and should be kept tightly closed in a dark, dry place. Similarly used Iodine Water Purification Tablets, effective in semitropical and tropical areas where chlorine is regarded as inadequate, are available at about twice this price.

Cooking Outfit

A cooking outfit is not mandatory for survival except insofar as it may conserve vital time and energy. A surplus army frying pan will do although heavier than necessary for this particular function. The high sides make it useful even for stews, and by using the plate-like lid to cover the food, the utensil may be buried in hot coals like a Dutch oven. If the army canteen is also taken, one may as well include the cup which fits over the end and which can be utilized in a number of ways.

Best of all if you care to go that far is a small nested cooking kit made of a light tough aluminum compound. Anyone who has burned his lips on aluminum will agree, however, that nested cups, and preferably the plates, may well be of less ardent stainless steel.

Greasy cooking utensils are easily enough cleaned under primitive conditions by boiling water and wood ashes in them, the lye in the latter combining with the fats to make a soap. Natural scouring agents include sand, grass, moss, and the previously described edible rush known as horsetail.

Survival Rations

Fat, which in calories is the most concentrated food, is the sustenance most difficult to come by when living off the land. Butter, lard, bacon drippings, tallow, and oleomargarine have more than twice as many calories pound for pound than sugar and nearly three times as many as honey. In any limited survival rations you may decide therefore to include a preponderance of edible fats with the idea of completing the diet from natural sources.

Other concentrated nutriments to consider are chocolate, malted milk tablets, dried whole eggs, dried whole milk, and peanut butter. Rice, if you want a starch, cooks up appetizingly with a large variety of foods.

Although not having much food value, some of the compactly packaged soup and broth ingredients add what some regard as a flavor-lift to many wild dishes. You may enjoy powdered pure tea and coffee, too. There are numerous dehydrated vegetables and fruits, but corresponding wild components are generally among the easier wilderness sustenances to obtain.

You could also carry a small quantity of vitamin and mineral concentrates, although there would seem to be no ordinary necessity for these. If under conditions when you might need them you managed to keep going by living largely or entirely off the country—as you would probably have to do to keep alive—you would already have at your disposal all food ingredients necessary for maintaining good health.

Emergency foods may well be carried whenever practical in adequately marked waterproof bags. Any products best kept over extended periods in their original airtight containers you may decide to place temporarily in the survival kit unopened, with the knowledge that if bulk and weight should become decisive factors, you could transfer them to waterproof sacks included in readiness.

Rope or Cord

A coil of good rope will have innumerable uses if you have room for it. Otherwise, a few yards of nylon cord at least heavy enough to support your weight will not take up much space.

Toilet Kit

This may include one small towel that can be kept washed, nail file, soap in a waterproof wrapping, toothbrush, dentifrice such as common baking soda which has many other uses, comb, and any other small items you may personally want such as a safety razor and blades.

Repair Kit

The odds and ends of a painstakingly selected repair kit will sometimes prove outrageously valuable in proportion to their intrinsic worth in civilization. We all have our own ideas about what a ditty bag of such items should include. After years of adding and discarding, here is what I now find in mine:

A very small pair of pointed scissors, the best I could buy. Two rolls of narrow adhesive tape which can be used to mend things innumerable, particularly if in cold weather the tape is warmed slightly before application. Small pointed tweezers, also the finest obtainable, valuable incidentally for extracting thorns and slivers.

Cutting pliers. Two short, different size screwdrivers with handles strong enough to grip with pliers. Some nylon fish line. A coil of light snare wire. Rawhide lace. Tube of all-purpose adhesive, wrapped for protection. Rubber patches and rubber cement. A small file. Safety pins of various sizes, strung on the largest. A few copper rivets. An empty toothpaste tube that, with the pitch from a conifer for flux, will serve as emergency solder.

A small sewing roll contains a few coils of thread, various needles, wax, a couple of cards wound with darning wool, and several buttons only as these latter can be so easily improvised from materials at hand. There is also a small rugged can of gun oil and a few cleaning patches, one of which is tied to the middle of a nylon cord so that with care it can be worked through the barrel without the aid of a cleaning rod.

Here, too, is a spare store of waterproofed matches and a reserve compass, partly in deference to the observation of Frank R. Butler, for many distinguished years the head of the British Columbia Game Commission, that: "Our future will be as bright in the same measure as we prepare for it."

Medicine Kit

A recommended way to decide upon the contents of a personal medicine kit is to discuss the problem with your doctor, saving time if you want by using as a basis our general consideration of the subject from a survival viewpoint. The first aid kits commonly sold ready packed are not designed, as you know, to fulfill possible wilderness needs when any additional assistance may be days away.

Extra Clothing

Feet should be given primary consideration, which may mean inclusion of at least several extra pairs of socks. You may also want to consider taking some substitute footwear such as shoe pacs with either rubber or composition soles. Underwear, handkerchiefs, and other apparel that can be readily washed need not be toted in the proportions sometimes seen. A large soft silk kerchief may come in handy for wearing around the neck, for tying about the ears in cold weather or about the head at night when it is undesirable to dampen the sleeping robe by breathing inside it, for use as a sling, and so on. A spare woolen shirt always seems to be coming in useful.

Portable Memory

So as to derive the fullest benefit from any survival kit, you may want to include a copy of this book if only for use as a portable memory. With such a compilation of fundamentals at hand for reference, it should be relatively easy in times of stress to devise reasonable solutions for almost any number of survival problems.

To be sure then that this book is actually in the emergency kit and not on a library table when it is needed most, you or another may want to obtain a second volume which can be placed permanently in the survival outfit.

Such a copy would be inexpensive and practical insurance, and therefore a particularly appropriate gift for a son, daughter, sweetheart, brother, sister, husband, wife, and anyone else important to the giver. For one day this book may be able to prevent from becoming any more than an adventure some incident that, through lack of information, might otherwise very easily turn into a catastrophe.

It's Up to You

Survival in the final analysis is up to the individual.

"If a man does not keep pace with his companions, perhaps," as Thoreau suggests, "it is because he hears a different drummer. Let him step to the music which he hears, however measured or far away."

It costs very little time, money, and effort to be ready. If you are not ready, it may cost your life.